Memories of *Cowplain*

A fabulous story of the life, history and memories of our village, Cowplain

Written & edited by
Rosemary Wilson

TRICORN
BOOKS

Memories of Cowplain
A fabulous story of the life, history and
memories of our village Cowplain
Written & edited by Rosemary Wilson

Design © 131 Design Ltd
www.131design.org
Images © Richard James, where indicated
www.sharethosememories.co.uk

ISBN 978-1-909660-34-2

A CIP catalogue record for this book is available from the British Library

Published 2014 by Tricorn Books
a trading name of 131 Design Ltd
131 High Street, Old Portsmouth
PO1 2HW

www.tricornbooks.co.uk

Printed & bound in UK

Memories of *Cowplain*

Acknowledgements

Without the support from the following people this book would not have been written.

Liz, Sue and David at Age Concern, Cowplain.

My daughter, Sue and Rod, her partner.

The members of The Cowplain History Society.

Richard Blair, the photographer of the book and web site designer.

John Philips, the proof reader.

David Pink, for his knowledge of Cowplain in the past.

Tom Potts, my friend for his encouragement to write this book.

Councillor, David Keast, for his financial help

With thanks to

Councillor David Keast

David Hawkley

Dinkie Legg

Sue Brett

Jez Groom

John Gordon

for their kind donations

Original birthday cards from the collection of Dinkie Legg

Contents

Rosemary Wilson

Preface

I was born and raised in Cowplain, and it has always been very close to my heart, with many good memories and experiences from my childhood.

Over the years it has been an enjoyable experience living and working with the residents of Cowplain, hearing their stories and looking through all the photos they are willing to share.

In *Memories of Cowplain* I want to record these personal memories, photos and stories in book form, so that they can continue to be shared, both now and with the future generations.

So many thanks must go to everyone who has contributed to this intimate history of our beloved village.

My vision for *Memories of Cowplain* is now coming to fruition, although it is impossible to include every story I would have loved to in this book. Perhaps there will need to be a Volume II . . .

If you have any photos or stories that you would like to go in the "next" book please email: cowplainhistorysociety.com

We also have a *PayPal* account if you wish to make a donation towards the War Memorial which will be built in the grounds of the Age Concern from the monies raised from the sale of this book.

I hope you all enjoy reading *Memories of Cowplain* as much as I have enjoyed the experience of putting it together.

Regards

Rosemary
Author and Editor

In 1751 the name Cowplain was mentioned. There was a court case in which the Duke of Beaufort accused Mr Tooker, of Hinton Manor, of trying to con him out of his estate from Denmead Mill. The name Cowplain appears on one of the accompanying maps, [a little north of where the Village grew]. This is probably where the Spotted Cow took its name from later, long before Waterlooville was thought of.

Monumental Task

A little piece of Cowplain's past - its historic milestone is looking as good as new thanks to the Waterlooville Ratepayers and the Co-operative Funeral Department.

The milestone had become so weathered that it was almost unreadable. Lovedean, Cowplain and Waterlooville Ratepayers and Residents Association asked Havant Borough Council to restore it.

The council could not spare the money, and the ratepayers could not afford the £600 cost of getting the work done privately. However an appeal in the ratepayers monthly magazine for a retired stonemason to undertake the restoration caught the eye of the Co-op's Funeral Manager, Mr. Terry Myall.

He offered to allow two Co-op stonemasons to renovate the 150 year old Portland stone milestone, free of charge. The work was done by apprentice Andrew Gordon [20], of Southsea, supervised by retiring stonemason, Mr. Harry Bell [65], of Gosport, who has been employed by the Co-op monumental masons department for 33 years.

"I have never worked on a milestone before," said Mr. Gordon "it was very interesting, especially when the elderly residents talked to us about the history of Cowplain. One man in his 70s recalled playing leapfrog over the milestone in the 1920s."

The Cowplain marker

*Ariel view of Cowplain
late 1950s*

Memories of Cowplain

Local author, Dee Williams

It was in April 1964 when Les, my husband, myself and two daughters, moved from Sutton, Surrey to the brand new Hazleton Estate. The estate was still being built and we were the first to move into the nine-bungalow cul-de-sac of Almond Close. We felt like pioneers. We didn't have any pavements for a while and from our bedroom windows we used to watch the rats run around the other unfinished bungalows. There was another time when Almond Close was full of cows that had escaped from a field somewhere.

Our daughters went to Padnell School. Julie was six years old and a diabetic, and Carol was five years old. The school was about a mile walk from Almond Close and they said the school couldn't be responsible for Julie at lunchtimes as she was diabetic, so she had to come home for lunch. At first, I was walking back and forth four times a day and would have to take a pushchair for Julie, even at six years old, as by lunchtime her sugar levels were low and she was unable to walk back home for lunch. After a while, I found these continual journeys really hard in all weathers. I didn't drive back then and we only had one car, which my husband used. Eventually the Council arranged for a car to bring her and Carol home each lunchtime. I'm sure that wouldn't happen now. I did eventually learn to drive and my first encounter with motoring offences was along Hazleton Way in 1972 when I got my one and only speeding ticket for driving 45 mph. It was 15 pmh over the limit, so I had a fine of £15 and an endorsement.

Not many people had cars in those days so you were able to drive around the estate without having to negotiate parked cars. We didn't have any buses that came round the estate. The nearest was in Cowplain centre.

But we did have a milkman call every day and a baker three times a week. The fish man called once a week as did the butcher in their vans. We also had a fruit and vegetable delivery service. For the everyday things we didn't need to go shopping as they were brought to our door. We seem to have gone full circle with Internet shopping now.

We did have a parade of shops close by, which are still there. Hazleton Hardware, run by the Thompsons, a newsagent where my daughters got their *Tammy* and *Jackie* comics, a Post Office, a greengrocers', which always had a queue on Saturday mornings and of course the Crow's Nest pub.

We never had a telephone, but that was something we needed with Julie's condition. We applied as soon as we moved in as we were told there were some party lines, but they had all been used by the first phase of bungalows on the estate. We had to wait until they put a caravan into the car park of the Horndean exchange and then we had the new Roman Way exchange.

As the girls got older I needed to do something so I became an *Avon Lady*. One of the roads my area covered was Galaxy Road and I had one client whose husband was in the Royal Navy. She always gave me a very good order. Sometimes I worried that she wouldn't pay but she always did. Whenever I went in to her house I was amazed at all the expensive furniture she had, including a dining room table that was raised to the ceiling when not being used. It was years later that I read about the couple. They were Maureen and David Bingham and were spying for the Russians, selling them submarine defence plans which they left behind a post box in Surrey. He was sentenced to 21 years for espionage.

Nearly the end of the road

The root of the problem was simple, a growing number of people liked the place where they lived, but could not stand the name. Suddenly, Cowplain had lost its charm.

Unrest had obviously been mounting for some time when a local doctor, who was also a Magistrate and County Councillor, came forward with his revolutionary suggestion. If you don't like the name then change it, he told residents.

So began the celebrated, but long forgotten, campaign of the spring of 1934 when the correspondence columns of the *Evening News* were full of letters from the fast growing area, north of Portsmouth. The suburbs were spreading, and a new generation of instant villagers was making itself heard.

Dr. F. Beddow fired the first shot when he suggested to Cowplain and District Ratepayers Association that the time had come to discuss a change of name, from Cowplain to Latchmere. In those days, of course, such phrases such as "moving up-market" were unknown, but the doctor's line of thought was obvious.

He wrote: "I have long felt that the present name Cowplain is not quite worthy of such a growing and developing place. So many people are coming out to reside at Cowplain when they retire from business or the services that unless they visit the place first, the name may prejudice them from seeking permanent residence. In the centre of this district there remains the good old name of Latchmere, and why not adopt it for the whole area of Cowplain?" The association was cautious, but agreed to discuss the suggestion at its meeting.

That opened the floodgates. Before the week was out, five lifelong residents had put their name to an angry letter which gave it as their opinion that the majority of Cowplain people were happy as they were. Latchmere they pointed out, was on the outskirts of the district. Cowplain was a good old-fashioned name which meant just what it said - a more or less level plain in the Forest of Bere where local crofters had fed their cattle since the common land was enclosed 150 years previously. Just how many crofters remained in 1934 was glossed over.

The writers added: "Surely no one of ordinary intelligence would be deterred from residing here by a name which, after all, is composed of two quite good English words, and is, in our opinion, not more objectionable than the other suggested one, quite apart from the considerable trouble caused to the authorities by changing over."

This brought an almost immediate and scornful rejoinder from one signed "neutral", who recalled other suggested name changes, including Sunnyland, Berehaven, and Bere End. Most of the grazing cows had long since disappeared, the writer added, and the land sold for such exorbitant prices that the area would more truthfully be renamed Klondike.

Others joined in the fray. A teacher from the Senior School in Hartplain Avenue complained that they always had trouble when they took one of the sports teams to a competition of any sort. "They are inevitably described as the Cowplain Girls, which is a libel on their looks. All who know them will agree that most districts would envy the pleasant features of the children of Cowplain. The girls assuredly are not bewitched with bovine beauty. Would they not sound better as Latchmere Girls?"

Still the battle raged. A worthy veteran wrote to ask: "What ails the cow of ancient lineage and worshipped by some tribes as a veritable God for its abundant supply of life-sustaining food and drink? The plain, too, is a great asset, situated in the mist of hills. We, who have attained the allotted span of life feel very grateful for fairly level ground that enables us to take a pleasant walk without undue exertion."

Another correspondent supposed that soon the people of Boarhunt and Horndean would grow restless at living in villages which shared their names with animals or parts or their anatomy.

A desultory sniping continued for a while, then the novelty of playing the name game wore off. Latchmere and all the other fanciful suggestions faded away, while Cowplain, with its undeniably sturdy Anglo-Saxon ring, flourished. Those who had forecast that its name would deter newcomers must have watched in astonishment as it grew and grew. Sunnyland had arrived but in a different guise.

Gez Groom
Growing up in Cowplain
Early years

My grandfather and father moved from Portsmouth to Cowplain shortly after the war and bought building plots in Longwood Avenue, or Longwood Way as it was known. After the S-bend, next to Idlewood, the road was not tarmac but more of a track. This petered out into woods where Everglades Avenue is now. As more houses were built the local council decided that the road should become adopted by the council and metalled. A few residents were against this, including my father. All the residents had to pay for this to be done.

When Milton Road was constructed, the lower end of Longwood Avenue was built but was not joined with the other part of Longwood Avenue. For a while a field, where the lower S-bend is, kept the two parts of Longwood Avenue separate.

As I got older and learnt how to ride a bike, with the construction of Milton Road, my brothers, along with friends and I were able to access the woods at Wecock where the two huge dips provided the perfect dirt track to use our bikes, as

The Urban District Council of Havant and Waterloo

HIGHWAYS ACT, 1959

NOTICE OF DEMAND FOR PAYMENT OF STREET WORKS EXPENSES.

Appt. No. 9.

To   George William Albert Groom

or other the owner of the premises   known as 43 Longwood Avenue, Cowplain.

We, the Urban District Council of Havant and Waterloo, hereby give you notice that we demand of you payment of the sum of £119 .14 . 5   being the amount of the expenses incurred by us (and remaining owing) in respect of the above-mentioned premises in the execution of street works in Longwood Avenue, Cowplain, together with interest on such sum at the rate of five and three-quarters pounds per cent per annum from the date of the final apportionment (viz. 23rd February, 1960) until payment is made.

Dated this Twenty-third day of February, 1960.

Clerk of the Council.

Town Hall,
Havant,
Hants.

did many other young Cowplain boys. Another good place to test our skills were the 'Humps and Bumps' at the end of Padnell Road, next to Borrow's 'Padnell Grange'. As we got older the bikes were replaced with a motor scooter - heaven knows where we got it from. Anyway, the throttle cable was not connected to the handlebars, so it needed two people to drive it: one steering and one sitting on the back holding and pulling the 6 inches of throttle cable. It took quite a bit of skill to gauge what the other person was doing, which we, most of the time, didn't, and we spent more time with the scooter on its side and us lying on the ground. But no real injuries.

At the end of our garden was a small stream to take away rainwater before storm drains were installed. When it rained these streams became raging torrents. The network of these streams were quite extensive, with the one at the end of our garden joining up with the stream that can still be seen running under Spring Cottage, which in turn stretched into what is now Hazleton. After having passed under Spring Cottage, the stream ran behind the houses on the south side of Longwood Avenue. Where it crossed Forest Avenue, a bridge had been built and the stream had a good supply of minnows and sticklebacks. At the first S-bend, it was joined by another stream that ran from fields behind Idlewood (now Passingham Walk). All of these flowed into the Latchmore Pond area, which I would think is the now part of the lower end of Durley Avenue. One area where the stream was wider and more accessible for us to play in and swing over, was what is now just inside Everglades Avenue. An elderly man, who we only knew as 'Grumpy', lived in a bungalow called, Barn End, which is still there but now extended (on the corner of Everglades Avenue and Longwood Avenue). He was always telling us off for playing there. Were we really that noisy and irksome or was he just 'grumpy'?

It was at this point of the stream that backed on to fields where horses were kept. In fact, one horse in particular, the dreaded 'Misty', a grey horse with such a mean streak - venture into the field too far and he was on to you. Too slow to scramble over the fence and you would feel its teeth. The reason you just had to run the Misty gauntlet was that going through the field took you onto Summerhill Road, which was a short cut to Cowplain shops.

Another occasional play area for us was the Queen's Inclosure. A great place to light lots of fires! But, oh dear, someone must have seen us and called the police. I'm sure all of the colour must have drained from our faces as we heard 'Oi! What do you think you are doing? Put that fire out!', and a policeman striding towards us. He took our names and addresses. I cried. I sobbed. I knew what would be in store for me when I got home. I delayed and delayed the walk back to Longwood Avenue.

In through the kitchen door and NOTHING. I think the sheer terror on our faces showed we had learnt our lesson and the policeman must have thought - no further action required. Think of the front page of the *News* if we hadn't been stopped.

At the rear of our garden was another small piece of woodland

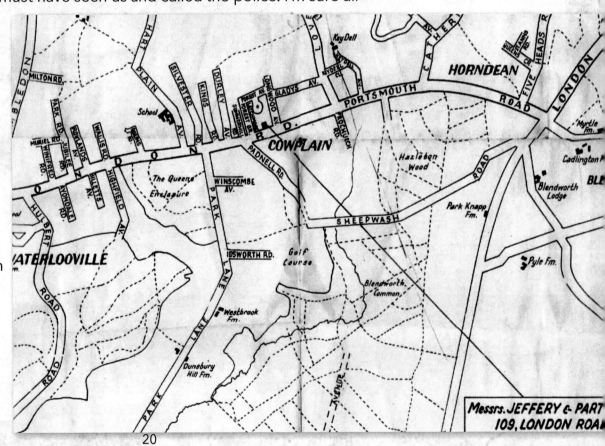

that was being cleared (now Forest Close), which became a playground for a while. In fact parked in one corner was a derelict tram from the Cosham to Horndean Light Railway, in green and cream livery. It was as rotten as anything but great fun to climb about on with lots of tins of some sort of white stuff. We thought it was tins of mashed potato, but again, had great fun smearing it everywhere. It was on this patch of soon-to-be developed land that we came up with another daring game. In the mounds of earth left by the builders, wasps had built their nests. The game was to see who could stand there the longest whilst using a stick to prise open the nest to reveal the Queen. Boy, was there a lot of angry wasps, but no stings that I can remember. I also seem to recall that at night the building site actually had a night watchman who sat in a little shed with a fire. Was he frying sausages or is that just a memory from comics?

One strange thing is that me and my friends, 'our gang', had our 'areas' to play in and never really ventured into another 'gang's' territory and they kept out of ours. Strange really that even as youngsters we were very territorial. Occasionally, there would be some confrontation with other groups, but nothing serious. It was usually just a stand off with comments such as, 'Well, my brother's bigger than you.' etc.

One event that took in most of Cowplain's population was 'May Day'. It's hard to describe really how busy it really was and Special Constables were drafted in. I know this because one of them cautioned me for having no brakes on my bike! To us youngsters it was the event of the year. The procession went on for ages. Started somewhere near Fodens, went down Silvester Road, along Milton Road and back up Lovedean Lane then along the London Road back to Cowplain. I'm sure the route varied at different times, but that is how I remember it. As transport was much more restricted in the 1950's and 1960's, it was more difficult to get to entertainments outside the village. The event took place on both corners of Padnell Road. The stalls and May Queen formalities were on the WI side (now houses) and the 'business' end, which we were interested in, was on the other side (now the Borrow centre and disused doctors' surgery). It was on here that the fair took place. Roundabouts, hoop-la, coconut shies and all that sort of thing, but best of all, Bumper Cars. All of this now just a memory, which probably just would not be able to compete with the entertainment available today with our transport.

The formula for our pocket money was 1d for each year of our age, so at aged 10, I got 10d (4p). Mind you, when I was twelve and getting 1/- it was enough to buy a fishcake and chips. To add to our small amount of pocket money we collected lemonade bottles, as they had a 3d returnable deposit. With all the new building in Cowplain at Hazleton and then Wecock, there were plenty of bottles to be had. The two brands were Corona and Hartridges. Corona bottles went to Smith's grocers, next to the Lobster Pot and now a house, and the Hartridges ones to Crosby's. There was a difference to some of the Hartridges bottles though. The ones from the Spotted Cow had a personal stamp on them and could only be returned to the Spotted Cow. It just so happened that the landlord of the pub stored the empty lemonade bottles along the side of the pub. It didn't take us long to 'test' if they could be taken and handed back to the pub for 3d. It worked, but we got greedy, taking far more than we could have possibly have bought. We soon got found out and chased off. The landlord moved the bottles to the rear of the pub after that.

For a short while I attended Sunday School at St Wilfrid's. I have to say, my heart was not really in it and my memory is scant as I only probably went a few times. My interest was more in trying to catch sticklebacks and slow worms down by Padnell Grange. We tried to keep them as pets, but of course they all died. The same commitment could be said of the Cubs. I went a few times but it just didn't do it for me. Mainly because my father helped to run a Sea Scouts group at Paulsgrove where they had a 'Den' with old sofas and sausages and beans on the go. Far more interesting.

Teen years

As we got older new delights beckoned, such as Youth Clubs and football at Fratton Park. Some of these needed a better income so paper rounds became a necessity. This was done at Crosby's, later to become Cantey, next to the Esso garage. I did three rounds: evenings, mornings and Sundays. The pay was about: evenings 8/- (40p), mornings 12/6d (62.5p) and Sundays 5/- (25p). The delivery area covered by the shop was quite a size. The easiest evening round was from the shop, up the London Road as far as Kendal Close and back down the other side and back to the shop - 15 minutes at a push on a bike. On the other hand, the Lovedean Lane round was awful. The last property on that round was The Bird in Hand pub. A long trek without a bike! The two people who mainly worked in the shop at that time were definitely two Cowplain characters, Pip and May. It was at about this time that I started smoking and occasionally for doing an additional round I could get my pay in fags from May if I was lucky. May later went on to work in the fish and chip shop opposite the Spotted Cow. I always tried to get her to serve me to get a bigger portion of chips.

Another trick to get additional cigarettes was used by a couple of paper-boys, (but not me, although I was happy to share the proceeds). To do this you needed to be at the shop well before opening, at about 5.30am when Pip arrived. He would go through the shop, open up the back door and go into the paper room at the back of the shop. Meanwhile we carried the bundles of papers and magazines to the paper room where Pip sorted the papers etc. He would then spend a few minutes reading the magazines and tell us to take the papers and magazines into the shop to put on the counter. A slow walk out of the paper room, then when out of sight a mad rush to the counter which gave you about an extra 10 seconds behind the counter before Pip ambled in. Plenty of time to scoop a few packets into your paper-sack. It did backfire on one occasion. As, let's say, Dave, was helping himself, he looked up to see a customer outside looking at him. Dave thought he was done for, but no, nothing was said.

When the Crosby's had the shop, they lived in the bungalow next door (long demolished) and it had a swimming pool in the back garden. When Cantoy took over, the swimming pool became full of rubbish and stagnant. One way to pass the time when we were waiting for the evening papers to be delivered was to put someone in a plastic dustbin and push him out into the middle. Great fun watching them very gently paddle back to the side.

With Cowplain School being only boys and Crookhorn School being only girls, one very important meeting place for us boys from Cowplain School, was the Smith and Vosper bakery come coffee shop (now Bronco's restaurant), straight after school. We would sit in there, with testosterone bubbling over, and wait for the girls to get off the bus from Crookhorn and hopefully make arrangements to see who would go out with who. As always, the more forward ones wasted no time and paired off, whereas most of us, like me, sat there not knowing what to say, drank our coffee and went home. You'd think that after a while we would give up, but oh no, each and every day we would be there, forever hopeful that one of them would take pity and do all the talking.

But the streets of Cowplain did prove fruitful eventually. Myself and Colin Turner were hanging around on the London Road by the Hartplain Avenue when we encountered two similar age girls walking along, heading towards Horndean. We started to follow, which became so obvious that we were forced to talk to them. They were from Wymering and on a sponsored walk to somewhere like Petersfield. Anyway, we followed a bit more, then a bit more and eventually asked them out (we were now the other side of Horndean). Having made the arrangements to meet at Colin's house the next Friday, we left them and walked back. The nexrt Friday evening, the four of us were sitting in the front room of Colin's house - only used for special occasions- watching TV. Eventually it came, the first kiss - well a full on snog. My, oh, my, she was more experienced than me. For what seemed like an eternity her mouth was frantically massaging mine. When we parted, my mouth and lips were throbbing. It was great. We only saw each other a couple of more times,perhaps she preferred a more experienced guy. Nevertheless, it had put me on the female map. Bring it on.

One event that passed through Cowplain that will not be recorded in any newspaper or gossip column, happened the week before 29 August 1969, and lasted for most of that week. A long trail of hippies made their way on foot through Cowplain heading to the Isle of Wight for the new pop festival. For a week there was a constant stream of young people passing through, none of them with transport, just walking. Some must have been walking for days, two were carrying a huge tarpaulin like a rolled up carpet.

One was munching on crab apples, which must have tasted awful, so definitely had no money and another was in bare feet. Probably for effect and showing off. I bet his feet hurt but he didn't want to let on. Like me, in my earlier days they were collecting lemonade bottles to retrieve the 3d deposit. So different from the youngsters today having pop up tents and the such, and getting a lift to the ferry. But they did make an impact on me and as luck would have it, where the pop festival was taking part at Woodside Bay on the Isle of Wight, friends had a caravan, so at the age of 14, my elder brother and I went to keep an eye on the caravan (we had done this journey many times on our own). We had no tickets but with the music of the Who, Bob Dylan, King Crimson and the Moody Blues so loud you didn't need one. What an impact on a 14 year old. In fact you could say that I never really came back.

Growing up in your teens in Cowplain could occasionally be quite fraught. In the late 1960's gangs became quite common. The skinhead fashion was up and coming and you also had a motor bike fraternity with a third group called 'hairies' who really only wanted to grow long hair and listen to heavy rock music. If you were caught in the wrong place wearing the wrong style of clothes, you could end up in trouble. At Cowplain School, skinheads took off and I followed. Shaved head (or just a very short 'short back and sides', granddad short sleeve shirt, Levi or Wrangler jeans, shortened by a turn-up (only these make of jeans would do), braces and of course big boots. The trouble was, living in Cowplain all my life, I knew many people who were my friends, some of whom decided to join in with those who had motorbikes and those who became 'hairies'. So my fashion changed frequently, depending on who I was hanging round with. Sitting 'on the fence' seemed to work as I kept all my friends whatever group they were with and enjoyed the pastimes of each group. One week listening to reggae and dancing with girls with with the fashionable skinhead 'feathercut', the next, sitting in a darkened room listened to heavy rock cuddling a girl wearing 'Loon' trousers and a mass of long hair. This was made easier as at the end of my school life, I joined the army, only coming home at weekends, which kept me out of the struggles within each group.

Once reaching the age of 18, pubs and clubs become part of the scene, although beer in the Spotted Cow was on the menu well before my eighteenth birthday. The Landlord would ask, 'Are you 18?' I would reply 'Of course I am,' and that was that. ' A brown split please.'

Many Sunday afternoons were spent in the long thin cafe along the London Road [now Goodview Chinese takeaway]. This was a greasy spoon with the added attraction of pinball machines which kept us there rather than the food. When it closed it was the Goodview that took it over. In fact, the Goodview must now be one of the longest standing small business names in Cowplain.

Latchmore Forest Grove, known as 'The Muddy'. Until the 1980's or so, this was a track with deep potholes and tyre tracks rather than a metalled road and was a short cut to our back garden via Forest Close. In wet weather the potholes and the road generally became impassable in places, particularly in the middle section. Do you go back and take the long way round when walking to and from school or do you try to skirt round the floodwater? We ended up with wet shoes and socks!

Cowplain Rec and Pavilion were prominent in my early teens. It was the Rec for football most evenings, even in the dark where we would play close to the car-park (much smaller back then before the Activity Centre was built), which had some street lights, our very own flood lights. The Pavilion was a great place to hang out generally in the evening as it had a sort of open veranda with protective side walls, which kept you well hidden, as there was no lighting outside, for drinking cider and female liaisons. Also, dead handy as it had toilets that were always open on the opposite side.

One forgotten set of structures that played their part in growing up in Cowplain were the wooden, shed-like bus shelters. They were great because like the pavilion, they had no lights so you couldn't be seen. Many a close encounter was had there, but sometimes, the ambience was unromantic if they had recently been used as a urinal.

Another meeting place was the Youth Club in the Youth Wing building in Cowplain School. Only on a Thursday and Friday night, but it was buzzing and packed. It was one of the cool places to be. You brought in your own records where you could hear them so much louder than if you were at home. They had a snooker table that really was just mis-treated, with a ripped cloth, broken cues etc. Occasionally they would have local bands playing at the club, which meant it was even more packed, just a heaving sweaty throng of teenage bodies trying to do some sort of dancing in a square inch of space.

The Social Club was also a good place to meet girls. As I was in the army, I wasn't around during the week, so unbeknown to me once, my friend Chris, had arranged a double blind date and we meet on a Sunday evening in the upper lounge. Her name was Carol Williams and here I am now, 32 married years later, which shows the Social Club was responsible for some very good things.

There was a waiting list to join the club and even with two sponsors, acceptance wasn't always guaranteed.

It was here that most Saturday evenings were spent. This is where I learned to play snooker, in particular with an elderly gent called Len Padley. I played him most Saturdays and never won a game, but he was always sympathetic to my lack of skill. Maybe that's why he never said no to me - he was guaranteed a win.

Space Invaders and Asteriods were two new games on the scene and the Club had them. How much money did we put into those slots?

Saturday nights was always a dance night, not normally a disco but generally an older band that played old time dancing, rock and roll and some attempted versions of what was in the charts. But, occasionally the entertainment was really good. German Beer Nights with buxom wenches serving huge glasses of lager, with the Oompah Band, encouraged you to drink more. Then there were the stag and hen nights (they seem so old hat now). We would gleefully buy our tickets brag about sitting in the front to get the best view. After our first 'stag do' we realised that we could be hauled up onstage. After that we, like many others, tried to find a seat furthest away, with others around us so we couldn't be got at by the performers. It didn't work, the performers didn't stay on the stage, they were in amongst us, climbing over the tables to grab some poor young boy who was desperately trying not to make eye contact with them. Was it me? NO, THANK GOD. Nevertheless, it didn't stop us going to other shows, and each time we went through the traumatic dread of being picked on and hauled out for humiliation.

Some of the entertainers were well known at the time, for example, Mike Reid and the Barron Knights. For me, the biggest name that appeared, twice, was The Four Tops. Anyone of a certain age will realise how big they were in the days of Motown and here they were, for a fiver, playing at the Social Club. Okay, they were older and all that, but they were good. Other big names that entertained us include, darts player, Eric Bristow and snooker legend, Fred Davis. Also, in the eighties, a few of Pompey's Footbal team who were members would be in the bar on Saturdays after home matches, such as Noel Blake, Mick Tait and Mickey Quinn. You wouldn't see that now.

The Casualwear clothes shop, in the once Mission Hall (now a hairdressers), remains a memory for one occasion only. It is where I bought one of my future wife's, first ever Christmas presents in 1976 - a pair of the most hideously bright, orange pants that were ever made.

The now demolished Police Station is where I have, thankfully, only had to visit once. I had to produce licence, insurance and MOT certificates. We had been to a wedding, so the drink was flowing.

One of our friends was far too drunk to drive home so I volunteered. Unfortunately his reversing lights had stayed on and as we pulled into the Social Club, the blue flashing lights appeared. I had to blow into the bag and amazingly, as the policeman said, 'By the skin of your teeth you've passed'. All we had to do was provide documents, which was fine as we had them all - it would have been fine if our insurance covered different people to drive that car. We were read our rights and later fined £100 each. It is these little incidents, early on in life, that ensure for the rest of your life you have the right paperwork.

Other watering holes visited were The Spotted Cow and The Crow's Nest. For a while The Spotty Moo was the in place for everyone. It was still two bars then and our interest was only the Public Bar. Friday nights were so busy that the bar couldn't hold everyone and we regularly spilled onto the car park. It seemed that everyone in Cowplain wanted to be part of the pub. They never had live music back then or any other entertainment other than the juke box. It must have been the sheer charisma, of the then landlord, who I can picture but can't remember the name.

The Crow's Nest was a strange pub. Definitely a locals' place, run back then by Ernie. To us it was for Sunday lunchtime drinking and darts. As you walked in, Ernie would have your drinks on the bar waiting for you. A sixth sense maybe, or was he just good at keeping an eye on the road outside and saw you coming. Were there times he poured drinks, placed them on the bar, for you to just walk on by? Probably. One older man who was always in there, his name now gone, but he only ever drank barley wine, and drank quite a few of them but they never seemed to have any effect on him.

All of these memories of Cowplain in the 1960's, 70's and 80's wouldn't be possible without a lot of other people who lived in Cowplain. I have mentioned so few of them. Some are still around in Cowplain, many have moved away and a few are no longer with us, so thank you to the following: Lee Jennings, Steve Ashford, Pauline Nash, Tina, Barry Ferguson, Val Leeder, Shirley Custance, Roy Maple, Alan Fleet, Dave Jenkins, Nina Hancock, Karen Westclock, Georgina Burton, Tim Smith, Bob Carruthers, Mick Day, Karen Bartlett, Lyn Smith, Maxine, Deidre, the girl from Hazleton Way who worked in Boots, Lyn Martin, Graham Smith, Colin Turner, Chris Gladwin, Kenny Scrivens, the Rees brothers, Mick and Steve Franks, Steve and Phil Neale, Cheryl, Sue Picket, Yvonne, Elaine, Gail, Kathy, Alan Forrester, Maureen, Phoebe, Garry Stout, Derek Spears, Sandra Pain and of course Carol Williams.

Although I now live in Waterlooville I am always in and around Cowplain and I still see it as it was: Hood's shoe menders, Carter's sweets, Faden's garage, Smith and Vosper's to meet the girls and the Queen's Inclosure, burning merrily away.

The Queen's Inclosure

Queen's Inclosure, Cowplain, is part of the old Royal Forest of Bere. The Royal Forest of Bere was created around the twelfth century to allow the Norman Monarchs to hunt deer and boar. It stayed under Forest Law for the next eight hundred years. The Forest had a court of Verderers who enforced the King's law and dealt out severe penalties to poachers. The only path through the forest was a muddy track roughly following the route of the A3. It was surrounded by wild woodland and was notorious for Highwaymen. It was taken out of Forest Law in the early 19th century, and parcels of land began to be sold off.

The best areas for timber were enclosed, giving rise to the Queen's Inclosure, today dominated by large oak trees and a few old yews. Cowplain began to emerge as village around the end of the 19th century. Local industries started up, most notably Brick making [around the area of the Hazleton Estate] for which the heavy clay soil was well suited. The Horndean Light Railway ran from Cosham to Horndean and a tram shed was built on the main road at Cowplain. Over the next hundred years or so Cowplain expanded into a thriving residential area, and became the very large village that we know today. *Wendy Buckley*

Library Petition Pays Off

A housewife's petition organised by Mrs Ruth Farnham of over 1,000 signatures has been collected in protest to the closing of the library in the W.I. hall in Padnell road, to be replaced bya 36ft mobile library which will serve Purbrook and Cowplain for five days a week.

The accessibility of the van is also a worry as people with mobility problems would not be able to climb the steps into the van. Mrs Farnham said, "of all the people I have asked, only three have refused to sign the petition. We have very few things in Cowplain, we should not have to fight for our rights" To this day a mobile library van still serves Purbrook and Cowplain area.

Save Cowplain library petition swells

A housewife's petition aimed at preventing the closure of Cowplain library is nearing 1,000 signatures.

"We pay rates, and there are very few services left at Cowplain now," said Mrs. Ruth Farnham, of Padnell Road, Cowplain, who has been sitting outside the library collecting names for her petition.

"Feeling is running very high at Cowplain. A lot of people, including young people, are very annoyed."

Cowplain and Purbrook libraries may be replaced with a 36ft. mobile library, which can carry 3,000 - 4,000 books and seat one or two people.

It will be in service five days a week, probably from Tuesdays to Saturdays, dividing stopping time equally between Cowplain and Purbrook.

No resident should be more than half a mile from a library stop. But many people are bitter about the possibility of losing their library.

BOYCOTTING

"I have heard people talk about boycotting the new mobile library," said Mrs. Farnham. "The elderly are very upset about it because Waterlooville is too far for them to go on the bus, and they do not feel they will be able to skim through books and periodicals in a mobile van.

"They are also worried about those who have trouble walking. The Cowplain and Purbrook libraries can be walked right into. A mobile van would have steep steps."

Mr. F. S. Baguley, the regional librarian, agrees that this is an important point. "But we have had a van like this operating in the area, and many elderly people have been able to manage the steps," he said.

"Those who cannot could apply to us to be put on the delivery scheme that is run from the library where an elderly or disabled person can have books delivered to their home.

"In fact the number of people who have been using the two libraries has dropped by a third recently," he said. "If this proved to be only a temporary lapse, we would have to think very carefully about closing."

Mrs. Ruth Farnham, of Padnell Road, Cowplain, collects signatures for her petition.

CONVENIENT

Cowplain library may be very convenient for those on the same side of the A3, but a mobile library will be n lot closer for many, many people.

"We have worked out about 15 stops for the library in the Purbrook and Cowplain area, and this will be far more convenient for many people," he said.

But Mrs. Farnham is not convinced. "Of all the people I have asked, only three have refused to sign the petition," she said. "We have very few things in Cowplain. We should not have to fight for our rights."

Fields before the Wecock Estate was built

First houses being built on the Wecock Estate

Wecock

Land was brought in 1965 to build a new housing estate in Cowplain.
* February 1970 Wecock housing estate scheme to build 1,400 dwellings rejected.
* June 1970 Wecock £6 million housing estate gets the go ahead. The land year was to be sold back to the
 council if not developed within 1 year .
* September 1971 The Lord Mayor of Portsmouth conducted the inauguration ceremony.

Community Centre

The community centre was formed in 1976 at the cost of £205,000 and was opened by George Best [footballer]. During the first year, the centre was run by a management team made up of Portsmouth City Councillors and representatives of local originations. Since then the centre has been serving the needs of the local community. In 2004 Havant Borough Council built and equipped a new centre as part of the area's regeneration project, and the "Acorn" centre was opened.

Wecock Community Association is run by a team of trustees with a broad range of skills and experiences. The centre is predominantly run by unpaid volunteers wanting to support the local community. The centre also has a number of paid staff, which help to ensure a smooth day to day running of the centre. They are able to cater for a wide range of needs and are happy to tailor their service to meet any requirements.

Keeping the estate litter-free has become a passion with Jean Reader and her group, The Wecock Green Gym, who scour the streets for litter. Jean was born in the local area so has seen a lot of changes over the years. To this day, she still volunteers at the centre.

Condition of station is criminal

Cowplain is unlikely to get a new police station for a least two years - despite renewed condemnation of the present buildings. A Hampshire County Council report to the county's police authority showed that £1.17m has been earmarked for the station in the capital programme for 1993/94.

For years councillors have called for plans to replace the cramped and converted station, which was originally built as three police houses in the 1930s. After a meeting of the Police Authority in Winchester, Councillor Brian Blacker, the Conservative chairman, said "Cowplain is on the Home Office approved list drawn up for 1993/94. If by any chance funds are available before then, and the authority was minded to spend them and replace the station, it could do so."

But Cllr. Blacker warned that this would involve losing the 51 per cent allocations towards the cost of the scheme the authority would otherwise receive from the Home Office. Councillor John Attrill, the county Labour group police spokesman, told the authority that the buildings at Cowplain were shoddy and "masqueraded as a police station." He was commenting on a report by Her Majesty's Inspectorate of Constabulary which described some of the police estate.

Cowplain station serves about 90,000 people in Cowplain, Waterlooville, Lovedean, Catherington, Clanfield, Purbrook, Widley, and Crookhorn. In 1971, the population was 41,000. Sixty-five officers and seven civilians are based at Cowplain, which last year recorded 4,062 crimes, nearly double the 1988 total.

A handwritten notice on the wall of the CID office states: "Attention. This is a hard hat area. Beware."

It was written tongue in cheek after plaster fell from the ceiling on the head of a superintendent. One of the buildings suffers badly from cracked walls. David Griffin, one of the two senior inspectors based at Cowplain said, "The working conditions at the station were far from ideal for the staff and visitors."

People reporting to the front office find themselves in a tiny room which measures only 5ft 4in by 12ft.

"The front office is cheerless, uninviting, and inadequate for the demands of a busy station. The first impression members of the public receive when they enter is one of inhospitality," said Insp. Griffin. "We are so pressed for space that we have to have a portable building at the back to house the officers lockers and clothing." Other problems included:

Having a telephone system housed in the kitchen of the CID house.

Administrative headaches caused by lack of suitable office space.

Officers having to brave the wintery weather by darting in and out of the three separate buildings to perform routine tasks.

A rest room which has only room for a television and about six chairs.

There are no canteen facilities.

Insp. Griffin said, "The conditions are a tittle trying, but Cowplain is a lovely family station. I think people have the feeling that the station belongs to them. Unfortunately the Police Station was never rebuilt; it was closed and the building was made into flats."

Murder in Cowplain

Christmas Eve 1968 or 1969 a man was stabbed in the forcourt of the Rainbow Public House in Milton Road. The licensee at the time was Mr Irons.

For many years the sergeant in charge of Cowplain Police Station was Mr Jim Hope.

When I joined the C.I.D. at the station there was only one detective working there. When I left, there were 6 Detective Constables and one Detective Sergeant. Crime had increased considerably ! !

In the sixties the area was patrolled in a grey and white Hillman Husky.

Eileen Gordon worked at the station for 26 years.

Ray Piper

LONDON ROAD SOUTH, COWPLAIN.

Top of Silvester Road then: Pinetree stores 1950s, 4 private houses

Top of Silvester Road now: One of the original trees still remains

Greetings I send to thee
Wishes extend to thee,
Knowing thy worth.
May'st thou have more of these
Yea, a great store of these
Days of thy birth.

Best Wishes

*All new images in this section
courtesy Richard James*

Now: *Carpet shop; Curves; Hairdressers*

The Foden Works were here from 1930s - 1950s;
Waitrose & Bank to 1960s.

Now: *Lidls; Fish & Chip shop*
All new photos in the section © R James

Car shed Lane Post Office circa 1900s

Shopkeepers in Cowplain

Mr Dust, known as "Dusty" for obvious reasons, had his general store set up in his front room on the corner of Silvester Road. He used to freeze orange squash in paper cups, {in the summer} and sell them to us children for 2d. They used to last for hours. Mr & Mrs Hearns ran Smeeds off-licence, Mrs Hearn would make toffee apples, the "bush telegraph" would tell us children when they were ready, and we would troop round to the back door to buy one for 6d.

Michael Tarrant

Ariel view of the Foden Works

Now left: *Co-Op Funeral Directors*
Then: *Boots the Ironmongers 1950s; Greengrocer; Florist.*
    Above: *Dentist*
Now right: *Sue Ryder Charity Shop*
Then: *Pook's Newsagent 1950s; Coxen's Newsagent; Gifts; Cycle Shop.*

Now *l to r: Barclays Bank; Insurance Broker; Cafe; Italian Restaurant*
Then: *Private house; Cowle's Butcher and Harcourt's Grocery/ Post Office 1940s-'50s; Pink's supermarket; Bargain Shop; Spar Grocers*

Harcourt's Grocery/ Post Office 1940s-'50s; Maytree Cottage

Now: *Red Lounge Restaurant;* Then: *Maytree Cottage '30s-'60s*

Now: *Restaurant*

King's Road

In King's Road Pyle's Builder is now a Beauty Shop. Snook's Drapers 1930s, later included Post Office is now Dentist and Dry Cleaners.

Then: *Kile's Grocers*

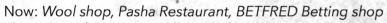

Now: *Wool shop, Pasha Restaurant, BETFRED Betting shop*
Then: *Gauntlet's Dairy and private houses*

Now left: *Booze & More*
Then: *Grant's Off Licence; Smeed's Off Licence*
Now right: *Corbier Ladies Hairdresser, Gino's Gentlemen's Hairdressers in the back*
Then: *The Mission*

BROADWAY, COWPLAIN.

Now: *Estate Agents; Weston's Chemist, Tucker's Chemist; Chinese Take Away; Rowan's Charity Shop; Palash Tandoori Restaurant; Hiedi's*
Then: *Private houses, then Reg Tilly Tailor; Frank Stockers Band; Thomas Barbers; Tumblers Radio & Cycle Shop; Self-fit Car Spares*
shop Butler's Electricty, then Chapman's Laundry (composite photo)

How about Les Simpson the barber? asks *Jez Groom*

When I was younger and went there for my short back and sides he didn't have a modern chair that went up and down. For us kids, he put a plank of wood across the arms of the chair and we sat on that.

I have never seen anyone who used scissors like him. Even when he wasn't cutting your hair, if he had scissors in his hand they were continually going 'snip, snip, snip', like an involuntary action. As we got older and progressed to sit in the chair proper, it was still short back and sides with the ever repeated comment at the end, "There you go 'andsome," while I was inwardly sniggering at the carton of Durex on the side.

Round about the age of 13 or 14, a new barber opened up, Brown's. He was dearer than Les Simpson but, oh joy, he would cut your hair in the much wanted Boston cut. You felt so 'Chic' with a Boston haircut (square cut at the back instead of shaved straight up).

Now from left: *Arnold's Optician; Upholstery & Curtain Making; Funnel's Estate Agents*
Then: *Burden's Chemist; Hood's Cobbler; Mrs Burden's Hairdressers*

On the corner of Durley Avenue, now the Tax Shop

Sweet couple kept door ajar on Yesterday

Les and Sylvia Carter have been selling sweets from their old fashion shop in Cowplain since 1957. They supplied aniseed balls and pear drops, about 18,000 sweets in all to the Royal Navy during the Falklands' conflict. Apparently it serves as a morale booster to have a taste of home when you are so far away. The affection friends and customers have for the business was obvious when they staged a surprise party for the husband and wife on their final day in the shop in [1997].

Sylvia said, "Our customers tell us that there is something quite romantic about stepping through the shop door into a world where sweets are still measured out in ounces and pounds, from huge jars."

Dolly mixtures and jelly babies were firm favourites in 1957 and still are now. But 40 years ago a quarter of a pound would have cost the equivalent of two and half pence - now it will set you back 56p.

One special retirement letter came from Jean and Ray Harding of Cowplain. They said, "We came to Cowplain in 1960 and our three children loved their visits to Carter's. You were so patient when they were choosing their sweets and so helpful too regarding our own special favourites."

Les said, "Our friend Pearl Wood is now running the business and I'm sure it will continue in safe hands for many years to come."

C.W. Tumber

"My maiden name was Tumber, and I lived at 45, Hartplain Avenue. I attended the Hartplain Infants and Junior school, where Mr Watson was head teacher. I then went onto Cowplain, Secondary Modern school.

My father was a local trader, C W J Tumber, starting initially from home and then progressing to his first shop in 1946 in Cowplain, selling toys, radios, tvs, white goods and electrical equipment. He later moved to the corner of Durley Avenue, which had been Kimble cake shop, where he stayed until his retirement in 1981, at the age of 60.

The shop was the centre of my world. After school and at weekends, I would help in the shop and on leaving school I worked there full time. After I married and had a family, I worked part time.

My father was also a member of the Waterlooville Motorcycle Club."

Susan McKee [née Tumber]

Mr Charles WJ Tumber his first radio shop in London Road, Cowplain about 1946

77 London Road, inside Tumber's TV/Radio Shop

Tumber's Electrical shop on the corner of Durley Avenue (now the Tax Shop), was a big draw for children. Not the electrical goods on display in the main shop window, but a side window in Durley Avenue where the latest Corgi and Dinky toys were on show. In particular was James Bond's gold Aston Martin DBS from Goldfinger. It was the must have Christmas present in the mid 1960's and cost 9/lld (just under 50p). I did get one but not from Tumber's as they had sold out. It meant a trip to Sidney Keast's toy shop in the metropolis of Waterlooville.

Carter's, like everyone else for decades, was the place for every sort of sweet. Although there were a few newsagents that sold the fashionable sweets of the day, it was Carter's where you went for something special.

On the corner of Silvester Road was Pinetree Stores run by Mr Dust. The reason I mention him? His was the only place in Cowplain where you could buy single cigarettes. He would quite happily split up a packet of Park Drive for us 14 year olds. He was also quick to chase you down Silvester Road when he caught you pinching sweets.

Heath's grocers (now the KFC takeaway), will be mentioned by many, but for me it was the old railway carriage behind the shop where he appeared to live. Also, the huge barns where he kept his hundreds or even thousands of chickens. What a racket they made. He was proud to have been the supplier of eggs to Chay Blyth for his round the world sailing trip. He had a large hand painted sign for many months outside his shop stating:

'I supplied eggs to Chay Blyth.'

Durley Avenue

Now: *Motor Cycle shop; Co-op store; Alison's Florist; Accountants*
Then: *Wadham's Garage Tractor Repair shop & Petrol Station; Singleton's Coal Yard; Durley Drapery;*
Bon-Bon Sweet Shop and Book Lending (composite photo)

Summerhill Road

Now: Private houses
Then: Passingham's Builders Yard and Harcourt's yard

Latchmore Forest Grove

Now: Accountants
Then: Steers Transport Cafe

Now: South Coast Exotic
Then: Reed's Painter & Decorator, Llyods Bank

Now: Pimm's Newsagents
Then: Leslie's Taxis [also Ran Dance Band]
Then: Shackleton, Bolt's, Crosby, Cantoy - all newsagents

Now: Collinson's Garage and Petrol Station, Spotted Cow
    Public House, Doctor's surgery
Then: Silvester's Garage and Petrol Station, Tilly's
    reclamation yard at back

Now: South Coast Exotic
Then: Reed's Painter & Decorator, Llyods Bank

Longwood Avenue

Now: Kentucky Takeaway
Then: Bettaworks Fencing
Then: Heath's Bakery and General Stores

Now: Private Houses
Then: Mr Vosey the cobler, Johnson Carrier
Then: F. J. W. Electrical Repair Shop
Then: Hillview School

Now: Pimm's Newsagents
Then: Shackleton, Bolt's, Crosby,
Cantoy - all Newsagents

51

Heath's Bakery and General Store

Harry Heath was one of the first shop keepers in Cowplain. He kept chickens in the back garden to supply eggs to sell in the shop and when they died he also sold them.

After the Second World War, his bakery was so successful that he added a cake oven to meet the demand. Fuel for the old wood oven came as *Bunts* [faggots of brushwood], supplied from Clanfield coppice. Flour came from Batley Mills and was kept in the loft over the bake house. Wooden topped bins were used as storage and work surfaces. Large mobile racks held all the bread and cakes, and grocery orders. Between the bake house and the shop was the loading shed for the vans.

1950s shopping for food was a daily task. Cheese, butter, bacon and biscuits were prepared to order and wrapped in greaseproof paper or put into paper bags. A small loaf of bread cost 4 1/4d, a large, 7 1/2d and 8d to get it sliced & wrapped. It was delivered three times a week, going as far as the Hog's Lodge and the Bat and Ball public houses. Customers could order groceries, which were sent out two days later, free of charge. The bakery closed in the mid 1950s and the shop closed several years later.

It had been used by several business's before it became Kentucky Fried Chicken.   *Jane Heath*

Forest and East View, Cowplain.

Harry Heath Grocers & Bake House. Built late 1800s

October 1970
   Chay Blyth needed three dozen eggs under 24 hours old .This was for his round the world trip. As Harry still kept chickens he was able to supply them.
   Chay's wife came early morning to collect the eggs, which were then painted with a preservative. After the trip was completed a letter of thanks and a signed copy of his book was received by Harry.
Jane Heath

1 Laurel Villas.
Providence Hill.
Bursledon.
Southampton.

Dear Mr. Egg man.

My apologies for your title but we do not know your name.

In Oct. 1970 you kindly gave me 30 odd eggs for my voyage around the world. You asked for me to keep the last six shells and blow out the eggs. I did this and brought them home intact. Unfortunately, when unloading the boat they got broken.

Due to many things, mainly a comprehensive lecture tour I have been unable to get over to see you to explain.

2

I enclose one of my books 'The Impossible Voyage' - I hope it will compensate a little for the loss of the eggs.

Thank you indeed for your kindness the eggs were very much appreciated.

Yours Sincerely,

Chay Blyth

CHAY BLYTH.

Mr H. Heath's van
Body shells interchangeable to make tourers

Cowplain east side, London Road, north to south

Then: *Alma Garage [petrol and repair shop]*
Now: *Green Haven Retirement flats*
Then: *Butcher Braun, Durrant*
Now: *Men's barber*
Then: *Twynham's Grocers*
Now: *Fish & Chips and wet fish shop*
Then: *Private house*

Milbeck Close

Social Club
Then: *Burt's Pumbers*
Now: *Heating and Ventilation business*
Then: *W.I. Hall 1964-2005 and county library*
Now: *Private houses*

Padnell Road

Boys club then Doctor's Surgery
Now: *Cowplain Age concern 'Borrow Centre'*
Now: *The Family Practice Doctor's Surgery*
Then: *Police Station*

Park Lane

Social Club

J.E. Burt Ltd was a company specialising in plumbing, electrical and the installation of central heating. The company started in Portchester then moved to 38 London Road, Cowplain in about 1945, then to 44 London Road about 1954 to accommodate the expansion of the business.

The premises were situated at the rear of the house and comprised of garages, outbuildings, stores, a petrol pump and a flint bungalow, which was used as an office and games room where my brother, Rod and myself, Deirdre, challenged our friends to a game of snooker. The yard was also home to several chickens and a stray duck, which invited itself to stay.

Many of the properties on the Berg Estate were fitted out by the company and a lot of work was carried out for the Gas Board installing central heating. The company employed approximately 12 skilled men and 2 apprentices.

Deirdre Privett (née Burt)

Miss Miller's Private School

"Sunnymead School" was run by Miss Miller. It was built by Passingham's the builders and was situated in Summerhill Road. The Reverend Miller owned the school.

This photograph was taken in 1933 and shows Mr Hurlow with, left to right: Joan Merrett, Valentine Galipea, Dorothy Baldwin and Brenda Stocker.

Hill View School, London Road

In the twenties, funds were raised by Harry Heath, senior, to build Hill View School as an alternative to the state school. Mrs White and Mrs Grant were the first teachers and Mrs Bailey was the last, in 1946.

My dad went to this private school, owned by Miss Bailey. The school opened in 1922 and closed in 1945. This photograph on the left, thought to have been taken around 1927-8, shows John Turner sitting in the middle of the middle row.

There were no schools in Cowplain when I was young in 1938. The nearest was at Waterlooville.

My first teacher was Mrs Bartlett - lovely lady. The headmistress was Mrs Griffin - tyrant.

We were moved to huts in Waterlooville which had been used for the library. In 1940, Miss Pearson took us from Waterlooville to school huts in Hartplain Avenue, all of us in a crocodile line. The annexe opposite the senior school was used to house refugees.

At 11 years old, I moved to the senior school; it was divided into girls and boys sections.

Dinkie Legg

School Milk

The saga of free school milk for 7 to 11 year olds came to an end at the December 1971 Council meeting after many months of wrangling deputations and petitions, when it was decided that such milk would not be provided other than for those in medical needs. It was earlier in all junior schools and the protest against this was nation wide.

At least one local authority decided to defy the ban and provide funds for free milk from revenue and similar moves were made at Havant, not withstanding the fact that members may have been surcharged to cover the cost, having defied the current law.

It should be mentioned that Havant Council empowered to spend up to an old penny rate [approx. £18,000] should special circumstances warrant it. This built-in safety value is, ostensibly, to cater for an emergency. Providing that funds are not available in balances, that money can be raised by the introduction of a Supplementary Rate Levy. This can be imposed virtually overnight. Every householder would pay one old penny for every pound of rateable value [this would average about seven old shillings].

Not unnaturally the debate over the past 18 months have been more than tinged with party politics. Perhaps one could concede that this playing party politics with the health of children as pawns in the game. The fact that children need milk did not form the issue. I believe this was accepted as a valued part of their diet. But who should provide it? Is this the responsibility of the parents who receive Family Allowance? The number of applications for free milk belie this however, there being only 87 applications [followed by a medical examination], of which 17 were recommended.

The general health of our children is good and there are many contributing factors to this. Perhaps school milk is but one.

The Ratepayer Magazine, February, 1972

Cowplain Junior School classrooms were old army Nissan huts. Mr Watson, the Headmaster always carried a cane and used it. Anyone to be punished had to stand outside the office, and wait to be called. Not me fortunately but plenty of naughty children did. Most serious for me was a rap over the knuckles with a wooden ruler; some teachers made you stand in the corner. During the winter months we were warmed by the pot-belly stove. Mr Watson delivered the news that King George 6th had died on February 6, 1952 and we were all sent home for the rest of the day.

Shirley Dewey, from Padnell Avenue, was an excellent sports girl. She was offered a prize of a shilling if she could do a high jump of 4 feet, which she did. I hope she remembers this. We were both in the Cowplain Secondary Girls' school netball team. Marion Wooden, née Atkinson, was goalie. We went on coaches to other schools to play matches. On October 7, 1959, we were rained off and whilst waiting to be picked up by the coach we heard that Mario Lanza had died.

Coronation day June 2, 1953, the junior school held a party during the afternoon in the primary school grounds. During the morning we had all dressed up for a competition held in Waterlooville. I was a mermaid, long straw hair and a fish tail. The trouble was there was a lorry to take us to the park, which I missed and subsequently had to walk - it was wet as well, pretty difficult in a fishtail and carrying a mirror. I didn't win anything but enjoyed all the carry on.

The corner shop in Silvester Road was were our dog Nipper frequently used to head too, to get his own meat pie. He would nudge the shop door open then the shop keeper would give him his pie and tell Nipper to go straight home and not to bury it on the way. It had to have the wrapper on it otherwise he would not take it. Dad used to go to the shop once a week to pay for the pies. After Nipper passed away, our next door neighbour, Mr Humphrey, found lots of pies still in their wrappers buried in his garden.

Angela Falconer née Harrison [Australia]

Infants and primary school were in Silvester Road. Mr Watson was the head master. Originally the building was an Army Nissan hut left from WWII. Heating was a pot-belly stove fed with coke. In Hartplain Avenue there were huts left from WWI, these were used by the Red Cross. People made homes out of these huts.

In 1958 a new Infants and Primary school was built in Hartplain Avenue and the huts in Silvester Road were pulled down. Cowplain Secondary Modern School took pupils from Bishops Waltham, Wickham, Hambledon, Clanfield, Petersfield, Widley, Denmead and Purbrook. It was the only school for miles around.

Jim Starkey

Cowplain Junior School Late 1940s

1st Row; S. Husband, P. Hynton, A. Weston, S. Long, R. Hern,-----W. Kille, B. Burrow, ? Humpries, ------ V. Standing,
2nd Row;------? Forester, P. Hart, M. Carter, L. Waterman,------ ------ J. Churcher, F. Gehan,------ ------
3rd row; B. Pearson, A. Parsons, A. Wooden, D. Furlove, P. Woods, ------ ------ J. Turkey, C. Weston, A. Burnett.
Back Row; F. Burgess, ------ J. Harcourt, ------------ ------ J. Lawrence, J. Theobald, J. Shaker.

Do you recognize yourself as one of the missing names in this photograph?
The teacher with the group is Miss Stone

Above: *Cowplain Primary School, 1960s*
Right: *Signatures of staff at Cowplain Primary, 1962*

May 1962

Mr. Watson
Mrs. Watson
" Cowie
" Lockwood
" James
" Youngs
" Paul
" Hopkins

Miss Dambrell
Miss Sneed
Mr. Guy
Mr. Pead
Mr. Howat
Mr. Kirby
Mr. Cowan

Gilrs' School Staff, 1947 (photo Peter Colwell, pupil in the boy's school)

Miss Pearson, Mrs Grainger, Miss Hawkins, Miss Wright, Miss Batten, Miss Hall, Miss Mears, Miss Ash

Mrs Baker, Miss Haslehurst, Mrs Laidman, Miss Mullice, Miss Lane

Mrs Forbes, Miss Tout, Mrs McCormick, Miss Oliver, Miss Smyth, Miss Leach

Cowplain Secondary School 1950s

The head mistress at the time was Mrs Laidman and her secretary was Miss Lemon. Domestic science classes were taken by Miss Adams and Miss Fryer; it took a year to make our cookery aprons by hand. We also had head bands, which we had to embroider with our initials; we were taught useful things, like how to measure for curtains and matching patterns etc. In the cookery classes we learned how to make basic things like white sauce, various cakes and puddings. I have always used these skills as I am a keen cook.

The school was girls only. The playing fields were beyond the boy's school. They extended all the way down to Milton Road [which was not there then]. The playing fields were shared by boys and girls, though at separate times.

My friend Jill and I used to walk to school from Waterlooville along London road. Then through Jubilee Park across the fields to Hartplain Avenue and on up to the school. There were about 600 girls at the school at that time, as it was so crowded, my first class was in one of the changing rooms adjacent to the showers and main hall.

We had a lesson in hygiene and had to bring in brushes and combs to clean. When they had been cleaned they were put into a drying cabinet. One girl brought in her mother's dressing table set, [without her knowing]. There was gasps of horror from said girl as the heat had melted the bristles!

Colours denoted the house teams: Green - York; Red - Stewart; Yellow - Tudor; Purple - Windsor.

Some of the other teachers were: Miss Ash and Mrs Fergusson [Geography], Mrs Grainger and Mrs Grundy [Art], Miss Lane [Music], Mrs Heaton and Miss Mullice [English], Mrs Minter and Miss Mullice [Maths], Miss Hall [History], Miss Pearson [Religious Instruction].

Mr Metcalfe had the unenviable job of cleaning up after us as the school janitor. One treat we had was an ice cream from the Portsmouth Creameries van that came and parked outside the school every day.

Pauline Frost née Murray

Cowplain Senior School.

Cowplain School.

Before the lower part of Hartplain Avenue was made up, school children were given a grant to buy wellington boots as it was so muddy.

Play at Cowplain Boys' Senior School

Padenll School, 1951

Padnell School c 1965. School production, HMS Pinafore
Girl standing, RHS stage, facing audience is Sandra Pain. Girl standing in front of stage, RHS, with back to camera,
dark hat, white top and dark skirt is Carol Williams. Girl with gorilla mask in background is Sîan Jelly.

First day at Padnell Junior School, 1963

Rachel Madock's School

This school is now situated on Eagle Avenue in Cowplain, but it originally started in Bedhampton in April, 1971, and is a co-educational day school for 70 pupils aged 2-19 years with severe, profound and multiple learning difficulties and complex medical needs.

"Valued for being me."

Life at Cowplain Community School is a very hectic world, like no other modem day adult experience. No, the students aren't heavenly and yes, sometimes it's so crowded it's hard to breathe but it's probably the most free we'll ever be. The day consists of 5 lessons, each an hour long, 2 twenty minute breaks and a twenty minute tutor time at the start of the day. We start at 8:30am and finish at 2:30pm. That s 6 hours jam-packed with lessons that help engage all areas of our brain from compulsory subjects like English or Science (my personal favourites) and other curricular lessons from Catering and Hospitality/Food Tech to Law. Each offer a range of GCSE's or BTEC's to help us in later life.

When the school was built in 1930, it was originally a mixed school but later became a boys-only school as girls would go to Crookhom School. Then after World War Two, it went back to being co-educational but the genders were separated. Now, nearly 70 years later, it is still co-educational but we aren't separated by gender or ability, with the exception of Mathematics and Learning Support. The school also offers advice and support for a range of categories from college to jobs, to personal support for bullying and other issues, with Serena (our guidance counsellor), always lending a helping hand. As far as leadership goes, we have our new head teacher, Mr Ian Gates, (who replaced Mr Rowlinson who taught at Cowplain for 16 years), who is joined by our Deputy-Heads, Mr Brockhurst and Mrs Sewell. There are many extra-curricular activities that the teachers run after school and ranges anything from netball and rugby to revision sessions for all lessons offered at school.

On the physical school grounds, there are eight buildings:

Dickens Building that holds all the English, MFL, E&P (Ethics and Philosophy), and Law classes, the gymnasium, learning support and PSHE, the IT classes as well as reception and the fully stocked library.

Dickinson Building that holds the canteens, assembly hall, Drama rooms and Music rooms.

Sports Hall, fully equipped with apparatus for many different sports activities as well as changing rooms.

Brunel Building which holds the Resistant Materials and Graphics classrooms.

Schilling Building that holds all Geography and History rooms as well as fully equipped Catering rooms.

Conan Doyle Building where all the Maths classes are as well as Business.

Rose Building, not technically part of the senior school as this building is Cowplain Pre School.

The Business Centre is fully equipped with conference rooms and IT rooms to be hired.

There is also a gifted and talented group called 'Shine' that offers support for achievers of A and above who will need support when picking GCSE options and doing examination revision. They offer a residential to the Isle of White once a school year for these pupils to relax and "let go". We have a new rewards system called 'E-Praise' that allows teachers to log in and give up to three points a student to pupils in their class. We can then log on with a unique log-in and view leader-boards, enter prize draws, buy from the online shop and even donate to charity.

There are many trips on offer at Cowplain. In the MFL department, there are day-trips to French towns such as Cherbourg and Boulogne as well as long weekends to Paris and weeks in the Loire Valley, all are very educational as well as being a lifelong memory (going from experience). The arts departments offer an Arts residential that extends and explores your knowledge of Arts in exciting ways. All departments also offer trips all over the country from London Dungeons and The Tower of London with the history department, to Ski and Camping opportunities with the PSHE department.

In conclusion, I believe that Cowplain has its flaws but it is by far the best school that I could have chosen. I love this school, its teachers and its pupils. They are all unique and have pros and cons, but I wouldn't change them for the world. Cowplain has produced some very good GCSE results and I look forward to carrying on my GCSE's at this school.

Charlotte Hall

BIRTHDAY GREETINGS to my DAUGHTER.

My Daughter, may
your Birthday be
Surrounded by
a joyous host
Of happy
thoughts
and wishes kind
From all the people
you love most.

W.&K.
1386/3

The Spotted Cow Public House

The Spotted Cow was first mentioned as a beer house in March 1849. The original mid 19th century building of the Spotted Cow stood almost on the London Road and was acquired in April 1860 by George Gale, in partnership with his father, Richard, of the nearby brewery of George Gale & Co., of Horndean. George Gale bought,

> "for £240, two dwelling houses on the west side of the London road at Cowplain Bottom, then used as a beer house called the Spotted Cow."

In the 1930s the Gale's Brewery, it would appear, went through a period of modernising their inns and even replacing some of the older buildings. The Spotted Cow was demolished and replaced with a modern building with the new public house standing a little further back from the London Road than the original. Fuller's Brewery now manage the pub after they acquired Gale's Brewery in November, 2005.

The Brewmaster Public House

Situated in Hartplain Avenue, this modern style public house, built in the late 1960s, is currently closed and awaiting redevelopment.

The Rainbow Public House

Another modern style public house built in the early 1960s. This pub in Milton Road, caters for a wide urban area, close to the Wecock Housing Estate.

The Crow's Nest Public House

Built in 1963, at about the same time as the Hazleton Estate, this is another of a number of public houses that were built around the same time in this fast growing area of Cowplain. Unfortunately, like a large number of public houses it has closed and by October, 2012, a planning application had been passed to demolish the public house and replace it with four new dwellings.

Plough and Barleycorn Public House

This public house is situated in Tempest Avenue at the bottom of Park Lane [originally running from Bedhampton to Cowplain]. It was built in the 1970s, at the same time as the Hurstwood Estate, close to the site of Westbrook Farm. Until being sold off in 1936, the farm had been part of the old Leigh Park Estate.

Steve Jones

The Spotted Cow Public House

Dr Edgar Wilfrid Borrow

In the mid 1940s, Dr Borrow succeeded to the ownership of Padnell estate, which was then a working farm. He enlarged and improved the old farm house to make it into the attractive Padnell Grange and more land was given to extending the golf course. Dr Borrow was Waterlooville's Golf President from 1985-86 and his brother, Stewart, preceded him to the post from 1974-76. His most generous action was the 28-year lease of 30 acres of land to the club for the rent of £1 a year when part of the old course was lost to the A3[M] motorway.

He then channelled his energies into the milk fluorisation project and set up the Borrow Dental Milk Foundation to research the use of fluoride in milk as a way of making children's teeth stronger. This earned him an honorary doctorate from the State of the University of Louisiana in 1983

Dr Borrow was chairman of Havant Urban District Council from 1949-50 and was made Havant's first Alderman in 1974. He is especially remembered for the donation of land to Age Concern and the Women's Institute.

Dr Borrow loved his golf and played regularly with Bernard Daish, his close friend and Waterlooville's professional for so many years. Such was his interest in golf that he had several short holes constructed in the grounds of Padnell Grange so that he could proactice when his busy life allowed.

He will always be remembered for his good deeds.

This page: *The Borrow's house at the end of Padnell Road, near Waterlooville Golf Course*
Left: *Dr Edgar Wilfred Borrow*

The Davis family in Cowplain

My grandfather, James Davies, had six children, Zena, Alice, Kathleen, Bertha, Jean and one son, my father, Noel. They came from a village in Cheshire called Elworth, where grandfather worked for a company named Fodens Limited. Foden's had bought the Horndean Light Railway tram-shed in Cowplain and Victoria House next door. James came to Cowplain in 1935 as Depot Manager and moved into Victoria House. In 1936 he was joined by my father and by 1937, my Grandmother had arrived with their two youngest daughters.

Once settled, Bertha worked in Harcourt's shop .and became friendly with Joan Harcourt, while Jean helped with the office work at the depot and made several friends through St. Wilfred's Church.

In July 1940, my father returned to Elworth and married the girl he left behind, my mother Enid. They then set up home in Victoria House. I was born in 1942 at the Bransbury Nursing Home in Jubilee Road, Waterlooville.

During the war, Foden's Depot was requisitioned by the Admiralty and used as a torpedo store. They only used the front part, so grandfather and dad used the back part. Grandfather continued as manager and my dad had a 'reserved occupation'. He was not called up but spent the entire war in the Cowplain Home Guards, which used St Wilfrd's Church hall as their base.

I started school at Upper Mount School on the corner of Winifred Road, Waterlooville. A new episode then began when my father took over the manager's job from grandfather. By the time I was nine, I went to the Junior school in Silvester Road, moving up to Cowplain Secondary Modern School in Hartplain Avenue when I was eleven.

I had a couple of paper rounds at Coxon's where Mrs Sweeny and Mrs Coles ran the shop. I did Padnell Road before school and Park Lane after school for five shillings a week, [25p]. They were easy rounds until they started building the Hazleton Estate and the Cherry Tree Avenue Estate. The new roads were quagmires when it rained and the houses only had plot numbers. But the money went up to ten shillings a week [5Op]. The family had always assumed I would follow my father and grandfather into the depot and I had little say in the matter so I started there in January 1958.

My mother became a founder member of the newly formed Cowplain W.I., initially as secretary, eventually becoming President. In the early days all their meetings were held at Victoria House. She was heavily involved in raising funds to build their own hall. This included negotiating with Ed Borrow from Padnell Grange on what land could be used. Ed's sister, Mrs Payne from Padnell Road, was also a founder member. Originally he donated the plot the Borrow Centre now occupies. But the plot was not big enough and the building would not fit. So he changed his mind and donated the bigger plot on the opposite corner. Mum and Dad became very involved in the May Day procession and helped make it all possible.

By 1967, Foden's had decided to close their smaller depots and after 32 years ,Cowplain Depot became a casualty. They made my dad a Regional Service Manager, working from home and he bought a bungalow next door to Mrs Payne in Padnell Road. Foden's Depot, Victoria House and all its land was sold to Ed Borrow who had previously bought May Cottage and Harcourt's shop ready for redevelopment. He had already sold some of his land to build the Hazleton Estate, and Cowplain was beginning to change fast.

My parents moved with my dad's job to Cheshire where they both passed away, Mum in 1978 aged 60, Dad in 1984 aged 7l. They always felt their roots were in Cowplain and it was their intention to return and retire here but sadly it never happened. The Lidl's supermarket now stands where the Foden depot and Victoria House once stood and there is no trace of what went on there.

Two of my cousins [Jean's boys], still live in Cowplain and I came back in 1984 and lived at 4 London Road for 16 years. Although I now have a Waterlooville address, it's only a quick walk to where "the Depot"used to be and I still get a very strange feeling if I am in Lidl's.

Michael Davis, 2013

Michael Harcourt
Ol.08.1837 - 09.08.1928

Rented Latchmour Farm in Cowplain in 1879, while he worked in Gale's Brewery, Horndean as an engineer in 1878. 0ne child was born there but Mrs Harcourt said it was too damp to bring up 13 children, so 'May Cottage' was bought from Leigh Park House in 1881. It was an old hunting lodge with just two rooms down stairs and two upstairs.

The land it stood on started at the mile stone and went approximately fifty metres north along the London Road and a drop back [west] about the same distance. As the lodge was at the southern end of the site all Michael could do was build more rooms on for his family on the north side of the lodge.

By 1887 there were eighteen children, not all at home, my grandfather was the sixth child and in the army.

In 1899/1900 a builder wanted to develop what we now know as King's Road and to do so 'May Cottage' lost approx. 30 metres on London Road, 50 metres west and part of the extension of the house. The good side is that it was an exchange and Mr Harcourt received 30 metres on the south side of 'May cottage' this still left six bedrooms after part demolition.

Mr Michael Harcourt (seated), 91, Mr John Harcourt, 61, Mr Jos Stephens, 24 and Kenneth George Harcourt aged 10 months

John Harcourt
28.12.1867 - 28.09.1950

He purchased fifteen metres along London Road, by fifty metres west on this site. He built a house and a shop [grocer], also a butcher's and a house owned by Mr Cowles. On the closure of the post office, [which was in the front room of a house on the corner of Car Shed Lane], in 1908 due to the retirement of the Post Master, Mr George Grant, he had an extension built onto the front of the shop for the post office, after he took over as Post Master. In 1912 he passed the position over to his son, Edward [Ede] Harcourt.

Albert Harcourt
16.07.1887 - 01.09.1971

With his nephew, Ede, they were soldiers in the First World War. Ede passed the position of Post Master on to his sister, Elizabeth, for the duration of the war.

Elizabeth Harcourt
15.04.1876 - 26.07.1963

After the war Ede returned and took over the post office again until 1947-48, when Mr G Snook became Post Master. Later the post office was moved into the drapery shop on the corner of King's Road, it was run by Mrs B Snook.

Alan Butler, Michael Harcourt's great-grandson

Ernest Smith

My dad was born in Denmead in 1894. My mum was born in Emsworth the same year. They married in 1911 at Caterington Church and set up home at 135 London Road, Cowplain where they had 10 children. 135 London Road was one of four cottages, between the Spotted Cow and Spring cottage.

Ponies used to graze on the land at the back of the Social Club [which is now car park] in the early 1960s. My horse Misty used to escape, we had great difficulty in catching him. One day he ended up outside St Wilfrid's Church grazing on the grass. Reverend Eastwood walked up to him said "good boy" and easily tethered him.

When the motorway was being constructed in the late 1970s, I used to go through Borrows Farm at the top of Padnell road and through Havant Thicket onto the road that had a sand base at that time and gallop for quite a distance.   *Jane Wilkins née Carruthers.*

Jack Carruthers and Jane Carruthers were independent [Ratepayer] councillors. They lived in Padnell Road, Cowplain, from 1959-2006. Jack became Chairman of Havant Borough Council in 1974 and is an Alderman of the Borough. Jack is also President of the Age Concern, Cowplain. Jane was Mayor of Havant, 1993 and is also an Alderman of the Borough.

Jack and Jane Carruthers of Padnell Road. Jack was the last chairman of Havant Borough Council, 1974

National Federation of Women's Institutes.

"For Home and Country"

MEMBERSHIP CARD

COWPLAIN

WOMEN'S INSTITUTE,

HAMPSHIRE

County Federation of Women's Institutes.

I, *J.P. Turner*
wishing to become a member of the
COWPLAIN........Women's
Institute, in the County of..HAMPSHIRE
promise to pay to the Treasurer of the
Institute the sum of Three Shillings and Sixpence yearly while I continue a member.
I also promise to keep the Rules and Bye-Laws
of the Institute, and all Rules and Regulations
made for Women's Institutes by the National
Federation of Women's Institutes.

Member's Name.... *Mrs. Turner*
Date of joining.. *4.2.1954*
Secretary of W.I.. *P. Davies*
County Secretary

We were the first family to move into the Padnell Avenue Council Estate in 1947. Our house was on the corner of Winscombe Avenue. Where the Council flats are now were prefabs. I lived there until I married my wife, Maureen, at St. Wilfrid's Church in 1971.

I have many fond memories of the Padnell Recreation Ground, "the Swamps", "the Humps and Bumps", going to the Bon-Bon on the main road for sweets, "Joey's Field", the "Lily Pond", the "Boat Pond", the "Tanks" in Queen's Inclosure. Then there was the "Farm Pond" at Padnell Farm, where we spent hours fishing for sticklebacks.

Bert Steere had a transport café on the corner of Latchmore Forest Grove. The Cowplain Boys' Club was situated on the London Road towards Lovedean Corner.

We would have great fun playing havoc with the golfers at the Waterlooville Golf Club in Idsworth Road, after wading bare foot into the Golf Course Pond for lost golf balls, we would sell them on to the players.

I had childhood friends like Geoff Madgewick, George Verrier, Robert Pounds, Richard Silvester and Junior Knight. While at Cowplain Junior School in Silvester Road I was in the school football team and later went on to play in the Cowplain Boy's Club team.

Amongst the shops in Cowplain was a dairy, run by Mr Watford who delivered the milk by horse and cart, I would sometimes help him on his round. My dad was born in Mission Lane in 1912. The Mission itself was on the main road on the corner of Mission Lane

Sadly, I can remember the demolition for house-building of the Hazleton Woods, Wecock Farm, Cherry Tree Estate in Park Lane, [now Tempest Avenue], Highfield Farm Estate and also the A3 [M] Motorway that ploughed its way through the idyllic countryside that was our playground as kids.

Michael Dewey

Listing all the shops and people in Cowplain at this point will be duplicating that covered by others. so I will just mention the ones that affected me directly.

Idlewood is a place that needs highlighting, situated on the top 'S' bend in Longwood Avenue. What appears to be a small piece of woodland was actually someone's garden - the Palmer family. John Palmer owned Victory Brushes, which had a factory in Fratton and was Canadian. He was married, but I can't think of her name, but she was ill with liver disease and they had a daughter, Mary-Lou, who died in her late teens-early twenties. The house was clad in cedar planking, which gave it a log cabin look. He refused to have any trees cut down and had quite a few confrontations with the council as the dustbin men couldn't get up his drive because of the overhanging trees. Mr Palmer kept himself to himself, and although a prominent businessman, never took part in village life. In fact, I never saw him outside of Idlewood, apart from in his car driving to and from work. Occasionally, he could be seen, early evening, in a paisley dressing gown, walking his dogs around Idlewood, where he would acknowledge you. In the early days though, he did allow us to use Idlewood for Easter Egg hunts. Again whether he supplied the eggs or just allowed our parents to use a few bushes I don't know. In the summer months we could earn some extra money from him by working a few days collecting wood, raking up leaves and clearing ditches. It was always his wife who paid us and she was always generous.

They had a housekeeper called Hannah, who, when we were working in the garden, would bring out a bowl of hot water, carbolic soap, a towel each to wash our hands and a bottle of lemonade with scones and chocolate biscuits. They also had a gardener called Mr Stamford, who lived a couple of doors up in a bungalow, also owned by the Palmer's. Mr Stamford worked in Idlewood well into his eighties and was a machine gunner in the First World War. He always told us the same thing every time we saw him. He was paid a shilling a day and had to stand on a box to fire the machine gun as he was so short. He wouldn't give any more detail apart from saying, 'It was a terrible thing'. I can only imagine what he had to do and witness. When the Palmer's died there were no children living in the UK, only cousins in Canada, so Idlewood fell into ruin, with the house being burnt down, I guess in the 1980s. So what now seems to have become a piece of public woodland, it needs to be remembered that although covered in trees, is just another garden. As a side note, when my farther bought his plot of land, just a bit further down in Longwood, Idlewood was available but cost another £500.

One elderly lady to be remembered is from the 1950s and early 1960s who lived in Forest Avenue. Her name was Mrs Moule and she kept a few wild birds in aviaries in her extensive garden. The most bizarre was a magpie that talked as well as any parrot. How she ever became custodian of such birds is puzzling and like most things we never bothered to ask her at the time. My only guess is that she acquired them as injured chicks. Whatever the reason we would regularly call on her to speak to the magpie, but were never allowed into her house.

Jez Groom

John and Joan Turner

My Mum and Dad moved to Hartplain Avenue in 1945 with my twin sisters, Janet and Jennifer, and my brother, Richard. They had four more children, Ken, Gill, Colin and myself, and we all shared the three-bedroomed house, with Granddad Sherfield, (Mum's father). I remember Granddad smoking "Digger Plug" tobacco in his pipe and one of us children would be sent on an errand to buy this for him from "Pine Tree Stores" on the corner of Silvester Road.

My Dad worked at Prochurch Farm in livestock haulage and purchasing, with my Granddad, Jack Turner

In 1954, Joan became a founder member of Cowplain Women's Institute. She was in the choir and drama groups and went on to become President in 1982-3. She remained an active member until her death in 2001.

In 1977, Mum and Dad moved to a new bungalow, which they had built on part of the site of Prochurch Farm. In later life they both enjoyed attending Borrow Day Centre for coffee mornings, lunches and socials. Dad made a bequest to the Centre in his will, which helped towards the building of the extension.

Sue Brett (née Turner)

Angela Fallconer née Harrison (Australia)

The shops in Cowplain were the Hardware Store, next door, Coxon's the newsagents. There was a house and then the butcher's, a driveway and then the grocery shop, Harcourt's, where Jean & June worked. They used to have fingerless gloves on during the winter as it was so cold; the roof leaked when it rained and you had to dodge the buckets when getting the vegetables. The potatoes were always weighed at the back of the shop by Mr Harcourt. Can you imagine the kids of today buying a quarter of butter and 4 ounces of sugar? We were using ration books back then as well. I used to renew Mum's and Mrs Humphrey's from the Social Club on the main road opposite the Transport Café, by Latchmore Forest Grove, neither of them were very good at knowing how many points were needed but at the age of 6, I could help them out. I used to go shopping for Mum every morning on my bike before I went to school and get Dad's newspaper when I came out of school. I remember going to Harcourt's one snowy morning, coming out of the shop with the groceries and dropping the nine pence change in the snow, crying, trying to find the change. A lady came along and asked me why I was crying. She helped me look for the sixpence and threepenny piece to no avail, and kindly gave me nine pence. When I arrived home, lo and behold, the change had fallen in my shopping bag, so a profit was made!!!

Some of the residents in Silvester Road were characters as well. The Lampard's from number 14, Mr and Mrs and a sister lived upstairs in their house. They were upholsterers and they used to have Pontefract liquorice for me when I did shopping for them. In the row of terrace houses that I lived in, the Tarrant's were at number 11, Hatches nu,ber 13, Mrs Twyneham 15 - she owned all of them. Mrs Weston and her ancient parrot, 17, Elsie Silvester - she had only one leg - number 19. She also said that Silvester Road was named after her family as they were the first residents of the road. Not sure of how true this is. The Humphry's at 21, Harrisons number 23 and the Twynehams, 25. Dad used to call Ron Twyneham, Knocky Nellie as Ron was always doing things to the house.

Angela and Val New, 1959

At number 20 the Scoggin's home. They had an orchard - nice apples tasted a few of them. We used to do shows in their shed, telling jokes and dancing and during the winter we would skate on their pond.

At the bottom of Silvester Road was the Whitbread's farm before it became the Berg Estate. We used to go to a place called Bunny Rabbits playground and collect primroses and bluebells for our Mums. We'd be gone all day.

Dad built us a go-kart from an old door and put the wheels from a pram on it with just string to steer the kart - no brakes. It would take around 6 of us and we would drag it to the top of Silvester Road with everyone on board except one at the back, Mick Tarrant. He would give it a good push, jump on and we would try to get as far down Silvester Road as we could. We usually ended up by the primary school or at best outside Susan Reed's place.

Arthur Tarrant and my Dad, "Hoppy" Harrison, were great mates Dad was a self-taught motor mechanic. He used to maintain Mr Tarrant's Vauxhall Wyvern, he'd just charge for parts, no labour cost and each Christmas Mr Tarrant would supply us with a huge turkey. He was also an avid gardener and we received all sorts of veggies and the like throughout the year. Dad also looked after Mr Lake's, from Padnell Road, Robin 3 wheeler invalid car. Mr Lake was a polio victim as Dad was, hence his nickname "Hoppy", which adorns his headstone in the cemetery at Denmead, along with a T Model Ford engraved on it, his favourite car. He is now back where he was born. My sister Julie (deceased 2002), was born in the front room of 23 Silvester Road on 30th July 1949. She was a true Cowplainite born and bred.

We lived next door to the Humphrey's - lovely lady, Margaret Humphrey - and her Husband Will, who was the night-watchman for the PDSA. Never understood that he hated animals and ours were no exception. They had 4 children, the eldest was Bill. He helped in the garden. One day he was busy digging when our pet chicken, Clara (she used to knock on the door every morning to come in and lay her double yoked-egg in the Welsh dresser's right-hand cupboard, laid with paper and with the door closed, until we heard the egg hit the floor. She would then head off outside for the day), wandered on to their garden and started to eat some of the seeds he had planted. Well, he threw a fork at her and it landed in her side. She squawked and came running to the back door where Mum saw her and took her in to help her bleeding side. Mum saw red, pardon the pun, took out a rice-pudding, just put in the oven for our tea so not too hot, in its tin dish and proceeded to throw it all over Bill. They were both bound over to keep the peace for a year when they appeared in the magistrates court in Petersfield and a wooden fence was put up between the 2 houses!!! No more morning tea with Mrs Humphrey, who made the most delicious and light Victoria sponge.

Harry Heath Senior and Junior

In 1894 Harry married Alice Langtree whose family had a grocery & bakery store in the Causeway. This is where Harry learnt his trade. By 1901 the family had moved to the shop in 149 London Road, Cowplain where they had a thriving business. Initially bread was delivered by pony and trap, later several vans were used as the business and the village grew.

Harry brought the land next to and behind the shop. In 1908 six terrace houses were built on the main road for the workers at the bakery. Two years later South View was built by Waterlooville Builders, J. Edwards.

Tragedy hit the family in August 1908 when Amelia, Harry's niece was involved in an accident on her bicycle and died later that day. Cowplain's first fatal R.T.A. (Road Traffic Accident).

August 1909, Harry Junior was born but sadly his mother died age 39 shortly after giving birth.

Harry senior remarried Caroline Lay in 1911 and in 1918 twins were born, Lillian & Winifred. Caroline was 43 years old .

Fred Lay joined the business before the First World War, he went onto run the bake house and lived at 149 London Road.

1920 and the war is over and local business men meet at the bakery to discuss the formation of the Cowplain Social Club, which opened in May 1923. Harry senior was a founder member and president in 1927.

In the 1920s Harry and Caroline were involved in two local projects; raising funds to build St. Wilfrid's church, and Hill View School

Harry senior moved to the family house in Gladys Avenue. Harry Junior joined the business after leaving school about 1925.

1935 saw the marriage of Harry junior, age 25, to Doris Stride, age 27. They both worked in the business until they had a family.

Durley House Durley Avenue Cowplain

A nostalgic glance back to the turn of the century when Durley House was one of the focal points of gracious living in the village.

Mr Wallace Ash, a Portsmouth alderman and prosperous businessman, owned Durley House. It was later sold to the People's Dispensary for Sick Animals, which built its Solmar Animal Treatment Centre on the site. In the early 1900s Durley House was elegantly maintained; there were many servants, and entertainment was on a grand scale.

Mr. Ash built the first parade of shops in Cowplain [which are still standing today], retaining one for his own use for the sale of pianos. At least one of the Ash family must have been a keen amateur photographer. These photographs appear to have been printed using a process popular among amateurs at the time, in which the negative was placed in a frame over photographic paper and natural light was used to make the print.

Sadly, Mr Ash's business concerns later suffered serious setback. Durley House was brought by Sir John Timpson and like so many of the grand houses in the area, was pulled down for redevelopment.

Irene Connell

Durley House, Cowplain, photographed by Mr C.H.T. Marshall in high summer, in the heyday of charm and prosperity

Paintwork gleaming, spare tyre wedged into the curved running board, this veteran car, which owes much of its design to the stage coach, waits ourside Durley House for a family outing

I am Jennifer Ford

My maiden name was Churcher. My parents were Ronald and Minnie; we lived at 36 Forest Avenue, Cowplain. I was born on 8th December 1940 and my sister Mary was born in August 1945 (on the day the atomic bomb was dropped on Hiroshima). We were both born at home and the midwife who came to Mary was Nurse Button.

Our paternal grandparents, Fred and Mary lived in number 38. Next to us, number 34 lived Mr and Mrs Maglissen. Mr Maglissen was a milkman. Then there was some waste-ground, the Goble family occupied the next bungalow. Mr Goble was a bus driver. The Russell family came next. Miss Mole and her brother lived further down. Then came the Fielders; there were three boys, the eldest was Ricky who was just a little younger than me. I was allowed to play with him. Their house had an upstairs. We played in the garden in a double-decker bus. The Fisher family lived a little further down.

To the left at the bottom of Forest Avenue was a copse of silver birches. Mr Heath the baker, who had a van, lived down Longwood Avenue. Mr Heath sometimes took me back to school after lunch. Opposite us in a bungalow, was Mrs Attwood, then in Twelve Trees were the Charlesworth's; Ann gave me a doll. It had a 'china' head. Their neighbours were a couple, the man had been a prisoner of war in the Far East.

Mrs Blythe lived in the first bungalow in Latchmoor Forest Grove, (the muddy lane).The muddy lane has always been at the end of our road. There were red squirrels in the trees along the lane. People regularly filled the pot-holes up with cinders and bricks, but the holes always came back and soon became puddles after any rain. I had a mustard yellow coat. It was bought in Petersfield. It was a Harella and had tiny round buttons down the front, they took ages to fasten. When Mum and I were going up the lane I was jumping the puddles. She told me to stop as I would fall in, but I assured her I could jump the biggest puddle which was like a figure of 8. This puddle was at the beginning of the lane. I jumped, landed in it and was led dripping home.

At the top of the lane on the left was the Transport Café; it sold ice-cream. You had to take a bowl covered by a cloth and they put the ice-cream in it. It was horrid, thin and full of ice. If you turned right you came across the shops. Mrs Tree had the Drapery, further along was a Greengrocers; Mr Grant was at the Off Licence, Mr Hood the Shoemaker, then a sweet shop, Harcourt's the Grocers, and on a corner, the Post Office. On the other side of the road was the Police Station.

After the war the Welham family came to live

next to Mrs Blythe. He was a Naval Officer, with a very understanding wife and three children, Vivienne, Rodney and Nelson. There was a long hall in their bungalow which we children travelled down, sitting on a two-tiered tea trolley.

I enjoyed parties at the Welhams. Two ropes were hung between the trees in the garden, then a couple of men put a chair over the ropes and ran alongside the seated child. My friend Shirley Stephenson lived at 27 Morely Crescent. She had a big sister, Molly, a big brother we just called 'Boy' and another brother, Clifford, just a bit older than us. The V.E. Day party was held on the green in the Crescent. The orange juice was very weak!

Grandad was the Verger of St Wilfrid's church and would cycle (Grandad's bike was a huge black one and seemed really too big for him) up to the church to open up in the morning, and back to lock up at night. On Sundays he 'pumped' the organ and rang the bell for services. We'd tell him to keep ringing until we arrived. Rev. Force baptised my sister and me, and when he left, Rev. Seaford, or Seaforth, replaced him.

Dad was Secretary of the Men's Christian Association. I went for piano lessons in a house opposite the church. Grandad and I took the accumulator down to the garage by the Spotted Cow. We wheeled it down in a pushchair. Dad and Grandad played snooker in the Club opposite. Another time Grandma took me to see the films in the church hall.

In September 1946 I started school. I did not like it and would run home and be waiting for Mum and Mary to return. My teacher was Miss Stone. Mrs Busby took the next class up. Some names I remember are Stephanie Husband and Phyllis Hart. Her mother was a teacher. Their house was burgled and Mrs Hart was hit on the head. We had to go to the High School opposite our school for dental checks.

In February 1948, Dad was sent to Trecwn in South Wales so we moved there.

Doris Ellis née Sparkes
born 1917

This picture was taken during the Second World War, early 1940s. The Home Guard are marching at the rear of the photograph, they are marching up Hartplain Avenue towards the London Road. Doris's other sister was not able to attend the march as she was on shift work for the war effort. Kate Butters is leading the parade as their group leader. Dorothy Ayling and Elsie Passingham are carrying the banner. Doris is wearing glasses, her sister, Florrie, is on the right. Betty French is marching behind Doris.

All the girls did Keep Fit in the morning and Kate suggested they did Drama in the afternoon, hence the name "Keep Fit - Drama Fit". They performed at concerts and were very popular. They enjoyed performing at the Convent although the nuns insisted that they kept their legs covered, so they all wore trousers. The nuns spoilt them with tea afterwards and homemade cakes. The nuns had their own cow and chickens, so had plenty of milk and eggs. There was a little farm at the end of Durley Avenue where the farmer let them use his barn to practise in, on condition they concreted half the floor, which they did.

Jackie Forrest

1953 The Coronation
Cowplain joined in with the nationwide celebrations. These photographs were taken in Morley Crescent, where everyone seems to be having a good time.

Perhaps you can recognize yourself in one of the pictures?

Edward John Pyle

'Jack' was born at 151 London Road, next door to Harry Heath's grocery shop, [now Kentucky Fried Chicken]. Opposite the house was a garage owned by Jack's Uncle Richard. He had one daughter and she had twin girls, Pat and Pam. Jack was the youngest of eight children; three girls and five boys. Four went in the army and one in the navy.

It was the Pyle family who started the Social Club, which is still going today. Uncle Richard started as a chimney sweep but was successful and went on to own a good part of Cowplain.

Two roads were named after the Pyle family, Gladys Avenue and Pyle Close. Another was named after Jim Passingham, the builder, who Jack and his son Neil, worked for, for many years, building his own house from scratch.

Left to right: *Jim Passingham, Jack Pyle, Christopher Passingham*

I came to Cowplain in 1945 and went to Cowplain Senior School until 1946, after which, I worked for my grandfather, Bert Twynham in his grocery and vegetable shop, opposite the Spotted Cow. At a later date I worked for Mr Heath, the baker on the main road, opposite Alma Garage, [Hadaways].

June Twynham

Number 2, Car Shed Lane was where I lived with my parents and grandparents. My grandfather Albert Southcott, 1889-1952, was the headlines man for the Horndean Light Railway. The cottage came with the job. Car Shed Lane ran up the side of the tram sheds, [later to become the Foden Works on the main road]. Albert married Ethel Griffin in 1910; they had three children, Albert [Bert], Gladys and Nellie, my mother. Bert was employed by the Southdown Bus Company. Gladys worked in Harcourt Stores. Nellie worked for Mrs Snook at the drapery shop on the corner of King's Road. She married George Head.

I was born in 1944, after which they moved to Lawrence Avenue, off Silvester Road. At the age of 17, I worked in Burden's chemist. I lived at that address until I married in 1963. My parents stayed at this address until mum passed away in 1981 and dad moved into sheltered accommodation in Waterlooville . In 1984 dad also passed away.

Rosemary Wilson née Head

Copnor Cottage was built for James and Fanny Passingham to live in during 1892 by James Whiting, Fanny's father, a local Waterloo builder. Fanny chose the name because she was so fond of the little village of Copnor, now swallowed up by greater Portsmouth. James was born a few miles away in the tiny hamlet of Anmore. When he married he moved to Cowplain where he kept cows, had a milk round and worked as a carpenter and joiner for Sir William Pink's estate at Shrover Hall, and then for Fanny's father.

When the cottage was built it stood at the top corner of an eleven acre pasture where James was to keep his cows. At that time, the dresser was in the front living room, the brick-floored back room had a sink near the window, and cooking was carried out on the kitchener or range. Today's kitchen was then the dairy with shelves for the cream crocks and where butter was made.

Water was drawn from the well in the garden until 1921 when Albert James, (Jame's and Fanny's son) linked into the water-main run from the car sheds of the Portsdown and Horndean Light Railway, (Lidl's site), to Heath's bakery, (KFC). That year the well had dried up in the drought and water for the cows had to be carried from Latchmore Pond (now buried under Latchmore Gardens). James was unfortunate to have been run down by one of the first motor cars on the turnpike passing the house, not fatal but damaging. He died in 1916 and is buried at Catherington.

Albert James Passingham 1890-1970

When Bert returned home after the 1914-18 war, he worked for Silvester's and then for William Borrow, a local farmer and builder who had formerly run the brickworks at Padnell. However, in 1922 he went into partnership with his old friend Albert Harcourt, a skilled bricklayer with whom he had joined up in 1914, and they began to plan and build on their own account.

In 1920, Bert married Annie Hayward and their first daughter, Elsie was born two years later. The following year he was to buy Copnor Cottage and the meadows on which it stood, from the descendants of John Stares. After the four houses on the London Road, north of the cottage were completed, building began in what was to become Summerhill Road. This name originated from a rest camp in the foot hills of Salonica during the war.

During the last years of the 1920s, the Harcourt Passingham partnership ended but the separate firms prospered until the difficult days of the second war.

Fanny, who had stayed in the family home with Annie and Bert, died in1929. Marion was born in1928 followed by James Edwin, (Jim), in 1930.During the early 30s, a wash-house was built on to the back of the living room with a coalstore and an outside lavatory joined on to the dairy. This replaced an earth closet. A bathroom and walk-in pantry was added from part of the old dairy in 1937.

Age Concern Borrow Centre

Age Concern is a registered charity. A part-time manager runs the centre with the help of 45 volunteers. Age Concern Borrow Centre origins started in 1976 with a fund raising drive to provide a day centre as a means of helping the maximum number of older people in the local community. Prior to this, the Age Concern based at the W.I. hall was already running a club, coffee mornings and outings. Mr Eddie Borrow, a local farmer and land owner, donated a quarter acre site on the corner of London Road and Padnell Road, this is our current location, and why the centre was named after him as a recognition of this gift.

Fund raising continued, with large donations from Waterlooville Lions Club, Mr Borrow, Help the Aged plus an interest free loan from Havant Borough Council and many smaller contributions from voluntary fund raisers. Work started in June 1981, at the cost of £38,000, five years after the scheme was initiated. The Age Concern Borrow Day Centre, as it was then called, was officially opened by the Mayor of Havant, on the 16th October, 1981. The centre flourished and proved to be extremely popular, so much so that 21 years later, in November 2002, the committee approved a complete revamp.

This included an extension and improved facilities to meet the growing needs of the community. The amount needed was £300,000 and fund raising began immediately. Again some large donations were obtained, for instance the Big Lottery Fund £100,000, Hampshire Country Council £25,000, The Wolfson Foundation and Comic Relief £5,000 each Havant Borough Council £750. Plus of course many smaller donations from individuals and volunteers fund raising.

Four years and three months later £312,000 had been raised, which enabled building work to start in June 2006. Once again the Mayor of Havant officially opened the extension on 22nd of February 2007. Age Concern Borrow Centre is now able to offer much more to the community than some of the original fund raisers in 1981 could ever have imagined.

Waterlooville Golf Club

Waterlooville Golf Club was founded in 1907 when it was agreed that 52 acres of land was to be rented from Idsworth Estate on a seven year lease at £20 a year to 35 members. Mr Borrow was made an honorary member for his help in securing the land.

The course was opened officially in the spring of 1908. MrWallesgrove was the first professional, a position he held until 1914, Percy Long was the first Captain.

In 1924 it was decided to limit the membership to 180 of whom one third could be ladies. This limit was reached in 1925 and was increased to 200. At this time the first club rules were prepared by Captain AG Granville, the Club Captain.

Bernard Daish was the club's first professional when he joined in 1928, also as the green keeper and he remained there until his retirement in 1974.He was called up for active service in 1941. On his release he turned to his old job where he achieved 25 holes in one throughout his career. He continued to play until 1998 and died in 1996.

In 1936 Idsworth Road leading to the golf club was in a poor state of repair so it was agreed that the club should purchase gravel to resurface the road.

Mr Barker held the position of Captain between 1938-1945. The full nine hole course was open for play during the war.

In 1946 work started to extend the course to 18 holes. This was a very long and difficult job; the new holes were opened in July 1947 by the captain.

Lady President was Miss Mary Gauntlett [1967-'82].

In 1969 GE wood was appointed Senior Captain of the junior section, an office he held for three years.

In July 1964 an extension was completed including furnishings and the total cost was £15,000. The suggestion of a Veteran's Section was signed by 21 members. On the 1st September, 1965 it was received with complete agreement so the Veteran' s Section was formed.

In 1980, *The News* [Portsmouth], organised a 36 hole competition for the champions of golf clubs in the paper's circulation area. This first competition was held at Crookhorn and was won by Ian Summers, who was Waterlooville's club champion that year. In 1987 Waterlooville became the venue for the tournament, the name of which became the News-Waterlooville Champion of Champion's Classic.

1994 saw the 70th anniversary for the ladies. The theme for their celebration dinner was 1920s. Ladies attended in cloche hats and dropped waist lines. The next day an anniversary golf competition was played and this was followed by a tea, which included a slice of a birthday cake made in the form of a 70.

To this day the club is thriving; at the time of publishing, the President and Men's Captain is Graham Croft, Ladies', Gill Millet and Senior Captain, J Winzar.

Above: *First Club House*
Right: *Ariel view of Waterlooville Golf Club*

Founder member

Mr H Heath Master Baker

Founder member

Mr R Pyle Builder

Founder member

Mr Howe Master Builder

Cowplain Social Club

The first discussion of forming the Cowplain Social Club and Institute took place at 149 London Road, Cowplain, by four men, and when it decided to launch the club, these founder members purchased £5 bonds, repayable when the club became solvent.

The land for the club was purchased on the 29th March 1923, for the sum of £124 from Mr Borrow who owned Padnell Farm which stretched along the, A3. The builders were Howe and Bishop. Building commenced immediately and the club opened on the 23rd May 1923.

Produced by kind permission of Cowplain Social Club Committee.

Founder member

Mr Durant Master Butcher

FOUNDERS OF COWPLAIN SOCIAL CLUB 1923

MR H. HEATH.

MR R. PYLE.

MR H. HOWE.

MR W. DURANT.

The first billiard table, installed by Sir John Rowland and a Penny Fruit Machine Jackpot 10/-, both ensured the members' needs were catered for, although the fruit machine was confiscated by the Police as it was illegal, and it became obvious that other attractions were needed.

Thus, in 1924 an extension was added, consisting of a stage, kitchens; the first ladies powder-room and overhead steward's accommodation. Prior to this the bar committee acted stewards. This new accommodation enabled Wednesday whist drives and dances; Saturday carnival dances and badminton to take place. The badminton club was in Portsmouth badminton league.

The club, in common with other such venues, was used extensively throughout the war. In 1931 the adjoining hall was built by Messrs Harcourt and Passingham at a cost of £850. Called Cowplain Hall, it was suitable for separate lettings. Until 1940, five to seven year olds were educated at Watertooville Junior School, unless they went to Hillview. Quite a few German planes visited this area and one day a woman was killed by stray machine gun fire outside the Curzon Cinema. The Mums approached the authorities and demanded their children be educated in Cowplain, and from 21st June 1940, the Social Club was requisitioned for this purpose. A large cold damp air raid shelter installed on the front car park became the classroom during air raids.

Unfortunately a child was knocked over by an army lorry turning on the Social Club Car Park. The child sadly died and the school removed to Silvester Road, following the mothers of the children petitioning the authorities.

During the evenings, the Social Club entertained the troops, including the Canadians, before embarking to Dieppe and many of the hundreds of British and Commonwealth troops encamped in the local wood and roads prior to DDay.

When they left secretly, and at night, on the 5th and 6th June 1944, they chalked messages on local roads 'Thank you, Cowplain' etc.

At this time Saturday night dances were still held, although alcohol was in short supply.

Finally, at night, the residents of Portsmouth turned up in their hundreds and sought refuge from the Air Raids in Portsmouth. Young and old slept in the Club or in the air raid shelter. The President received hundreds of thank you letters, thanking the club for hospitality and care received by those unfortunate people. Around this time membership dropped considerably due to members being called up. However, lettings kept the Club solvent. The membership rose from a wartime low of 180 to 420 immediately afterwards.

Cowplain Social Club and Hall.

Cowplain Social Club,
Above: then
Below: now

How?!!! Fred Dinenage

MERIDIAN

Fred Dinenage

70th Aniversary celebrations 1923 - 1993

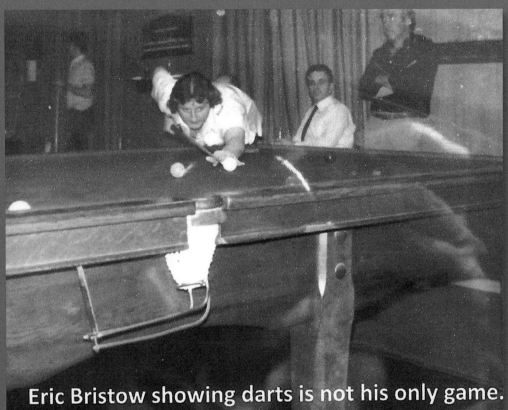

Eric Bristow showing darts is not his only game.

Cowplain Social FC 1964-65

1969 Winners six-a-side competition

W.I. Cowplain, 1975

The W.I. Hall Padnell Road

The land on both sides of Padnell Road was purchased by Mr Stuart Borrow in 1958 costing £500.

In January, 1963, Mr Borrow bought an army hut that stood on Southsea common, it was dismantled at the cost of £300 and in September of that year it was erected on the site for the use of the W.I. On the other corner a doctor's surgery and the Age Concern Centre were built. This land is only ever for community use and is never to be built on.

The opening night of the W.I. hall was on September 5th, 1964. It was put to good use by the members of the W.I. for their meetings, variety shows, seasonal fairs and as a social venue for the people of the area.

In February, 1975, as the photograph shows, they celebrated their 21st anniversary. Part of the roof was blown off in 1996, which closed the hall for a short time while repairs were carried out.

The hall was finally demolished in March 2005.

Cowplain Co-op Guild

Cowplain May Day, 1960s

EVENING NEWS
AND
HAMPSHIRE TELEGRAPH
PORTSMOUTH
COPYRIGHT PROOF

REF No. ....

Cowplain May Day
during the '60s

W.I. May Day, 1978

The Darby and Joan Club

On June 24th, 1954, the club was opened by Mrs Hyde, deputising for Mrs Chalis [who had broken her arm falling in St. Wilfrid's church hall]. They entered a float in the first W.I. May Day carnival in 1959 and all subsequent May Day carnivals.

They were renamed W.R.V.S. Thursday club for senior citizens and celebrated their Silver Jubilee with a party on June 28th, 1979. 70 members attended, with the Mayor and Mayoress of Havant as guests of honour. Mrs Sparrow made the celebration cake.

Cowplain Boys Club Football Team 1957 /1958
Back Row, L to R: *Mick Dewey, Tom Dyson, Bob Bennett, Mr. Foster [Manager] Terry Wallace, Jim Morrow, Brian Sparrow.*
Front Row, L to R: *Dave Grant ,John Gordon, Bob Sullivan, Paul Tweed, Dave Kill, Johnny Kill, Richard Whiting.*
This photo was probably taken at Padnell Road Recreation ground.

Cowplain Girls' Brigade, circa 1950

Cowplain Brownies early '50s

Our Brown Owl was Mrs. Alderton and Tawny Owl was Mrs. Jones; Guide leader, Jill. Dyson. We held our meetings in the old St Wilfrid's Church Hall in Padnell Road.

Back row: *V.Collins, A.Sherindon, E.Lawrence, P.Yalden, S Dewey, R. Alderton, M. Henley, J. Maclachlan*

Middle row: *R. Head, ? Champion, D. Pyle, D. Moon, S. Reed, S. Dyson, J. Tynham, L. Murton, A. Hammond.*

Front row: *? Champion, W. Gehan, J. Eddows, __, G. Patterson, E. Standing, B. Summers.*

A.T.C. 2260 SQUADRON. THORNEY ISLAND 1960/61

This photo is made up of Cowplain, Waterlooville and Petersfield 2260 Squadron. Can you recognize any of the unnamed cadets?

1st row l/r: _ Cooper, Paul Merle, John Lock, Tony Meads

2nd row: _____ Lewis C.O., Eric Coy, Roy Peach, Peter Salisbury

3rd row: Dave Willers, Terry Meads, ___ Bob Sullivan, Geoff Madgewick, __ Geoff Harris, John Gordon, David Grant, Geoff Burton

4th row: Barry Rogers, Les Jarman, Roger Bromley, Alan Hunt, Denny Horne, __, -- McArtie, Richard Brookes, Paul Castle

Back Row: __ Dave Petherbridge, -- Anderson, Bob Maple, Geoff Piper

Cowplain used to have its own drama group known as the St Wilfrid's Players who put on several performances a year in the church hall.
 Wendy Buckley

I joined the group in 1976, it had been running for quite a few years before this. We performed serious plays also comedies. Stuart Telford was the producer at the time. He was an ancestor of Thomas Telford, builder of the Ironbridge.
Eileen Gordon, née Summers

In the fifties there was a thriving brownie pack and guides held in St Wilfrid's church hall; I was one of the brownies. Also, there was a youth club running at that time as well.
Rosemary Wilson, née Head

St Wilfrid's Church, Cowplain

The foundation stone was laid on the 14th October, 1923, by Viscount Walmer M.P. The twin daughters of Harry Heath, Lilian and Winifred, presented the bouquet at the laying of the stone, dressed in identical pink and blue outfits. They were six years old.

The building was dedicated, on the 6th of April, 1924, by the Bishop of Southampton, but for the first five years of its existence, St Wilfrid's was administered by the parish of Catherington, and when 10 years later, Cowplain became an Independent Conventional District, parish church status followed.

The long awaited church hall was commandeered by the Home Guard during the war who installed a .22 rifle range.

In the '50s, there was a brownie meet each week in the hall and in 1961, the first scout pack was set up; guides were already meeting there on a weekly basis.

The Rev. Eastwood started his ministry in 1954, lasting 32 years. He was instrumental in setting up the Methodist/ Anglican project in Hartplain Avenue Church.

On the 26th May, 1962, the Assistant Bishop of Portsmouth consecrated the building to create the Parish of Cowplain.

St Wilfrid's celebrated their Golden Jubilee in 1974.

The Rev. Peter Hancock succeeded Christopher Eastwood in 1987. A generous legacy helped towards the cost of the rebuild and the final phase was completed in time for the building to be consecrated on the 6th October 2002. Buried under the western wall of the modern building is a time capsule containing 28 typical things from 1996. Rev. Dr P Moore arrived in 2002 with his wife Lucy; they set up the Messy Church, as a way of bringing families together. Around 60 people arrive after school each month and join together with fun, chat and craft, celebration and food.

St. Wilfred's, Cowplain.

St Wilfrid's, Cowplain

John Theobald, Godfrey Smart, St Wilfrid's, 1950

John Theobald, St Wilfrid's, circa 1950

St Wilfrid's Choir,
circa 1950

St Wilfrid's Choir, 1955
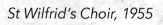

*Dinkie & John Legg, Rev. Eastwood (Senior), holding baby Ian,
with Godparents*

Cowplain Mission
now Cowplain Evangelical Free Church

The church has, over the last 103 years, been meeting in three buildings. The original tin hut was off Mission Lane to the right near the edge of the of the car park where it adjoins the back of the bungalows in Durley Avenue. No photographs of this building are known to exist but there is a painting. This tin hut was opened on the 7th October 1885, the opening address being given by Mr W Case preaching from Psalm 40 verse 2. Mr Case had been converted in April of that year, and he, his sons and two daughters were members of the church for many years.

It is known that the tin hut was rented but not much else is known of the original transactions the members did not meet to "form themselves into a church or society" until November 1896. From that time all the minutes exist and make fascinating reading. Incidentally, at the meeting the balance in hand was 12 shillings and 2 pence.

The church eventually, it was decided, that the tin hut, although extended on the sides and at the front at various times, had become too small. On October 17th 1905 a meeting of members was held which agreed to purchase the land on the corner of Mission Lane for the new building. A committee was formed, money was pledged [all details of which are recorded] and the project set in motion by the invitation of tenders for various aspects of the work.

The foundation stone was laid on December 9th, 1905 by Mrs Charles Dye of Portsmouth, although the actual building work commenced on November 20th, 1905. In a report by the *Evening News*, posted in the minute book at the time, the sum of £120-12-7d had been raised towards the total cost of £500.

The work on the church continued with Mr Smith being the Superintendent for a period of sixty years, until December 31st, 1938. Then my father Mr G Snook took over the oversight of the work.

During the war years the building was opened at night for people to sleep in as they came out of Portsmouth to avoid the bombing in the city. Towards the end of the war, many soldiers were stationed in the area prior to D Day and many friendships were made with people in the church. One such friendship still continues to this day.

After the war, the church began to grow considerably until in the early '60s the position became desperate for more accommodation. Various things were tried and plans submitted, all to be turned down by the Planning Authority, the site really being too small to extend.

Eventually land on the P.D.S.A. site was obtained and the present building was erected, the old building being sold for £7,000. It is remarkable that the new building is only a few yards from the site of the tin hut and so all three buildings have been within a few yards of each other.

The present building was opened on December 30th 1967, the foundation stones being laid July 1st of that year.

Peter Snook, 1988

I used to attend the Mission on the corner of Mission Lane 1943/44. Sunday school teachers were, Miss Greenwood and Mrs Pattertson. It was run by Mr Snook and the organist was Mrs Snook. Every Sunday morning and afternoon I went. We were put into little groups and read bible stories and sang hymns. We had to learn texts for the next week.

Wednesday evenings was Wednesday club run by Phil Able. We played table tennis and games. The evening ended with a prayer and reflection.

As we got older we would meet up at Boarhunt Church. We cycled there and the next week they cycled to us. We had outings, one to Butlins in Bognor and one to the Isle of Wight.

At the age of 14, girls left to go to work in, for example, service etc.

At St Wilfrid's, the vicar prior to Rev. Eastwood was Reverend Seaford. It was not consecrated for weddings and Christenings until 1930s, so I was christened in Waterlooville at St George's.

Betty Goble, [my cousin] and her partner were the first to be married at St Wilfrid's.

Dinkie Legg

MANY
HAPPY
RETURNS

Happy may your
Birthday find you,
And of absent friends remind you.

Farmhouse may turn into pub after all

Ambitious plans to develop Westbrook Farm-house for community use could be taking another turn towards a public house. Havant's leisure chiefs are to ask their policy-making colleagues to postpone buying the Cowplain farmhouse, until the possibility of a pub has been discussed.

The borough was going to buy the farmhouse from Portsmouth City Council to use as a sort of community centre,but after members of Havant's Recreation and Amenities Committee finally viewed the site, just two weeks ago, they realized the full extent of repair work which would have to be carried out on the building.

When the original development brief was drawn up in 1979, a public house was one of the alternative uses put forward. Now Portsmouth has applied for planning permission to build a public house on land to the south of the farmhouse, but Havant feels the house could be the ideal site.

"When we site-viewed the farmhouse, what I saw quite frankly was appalling. If we take it over we would end up pouring money into it from now to forever," said Mr Ron Beresford {Hart Plain].

"With the development going on there a public house is going to be a necessary, and I can't help feeling that would be an ideal place to put it. I would recommend to Policy and Resources to discuss with Portsmouth City council the possible use of Westbrook Farmhouse as a pub," he said.

Mr Beresford's proposal was seconded by ward councillor, Mrs Jane Carruthers, although she had reservations about the idea.

"One way or another there is going to be a public house there, but there is an urgency to decide quickly what should happen," she said. "Only a brewery would have the money to love and nurse this house, I would not like to see a voluntary group of people take on the burden of it".

No action will be taken on connecting the farmhouse to mains drainage until negotiations with Portsmouth have been completed.

Evening News, February, 1984

Cruel Collection

A pole trap, which it has been illegal to use since 1902, is among a collection of old, animal and bird traps owned by a Cowplain man.

They are reminders of the days when death to some animals was both vicious and cruel and when human trepasssers were treated with not much more respect.

The traps, some of them purposely damaged so that they could not be used again, have been collected over the years by 85 year old Mr Jack Turner, of Prochurch Farm, London Road, Cowplain.

The man-traps, strongly sprung with cruel iron teeth, would trap an unwary trespasser or poacher painfully by the shin.

Pole traps would be placed on gate posts or tree stumps to trap birds by their legs until they died in the vain effort to escape.

Another trap, for moles, provided a tortuous death when the animal touched a spring and released a set of sharp spikes into its body.

Mr Turner has, of course, never used the traps except to test one of the man-traps with a stick inside a wellington boot.

For many years, the traps were among a collection of old farm implements on display at The Farmer, public house, Catherington, which Mr Turner ran for 38 years.

His collection of old farming implements also includes shepherds' crooks which are more than 100 years old, a cows' drinking horn dated 1829, and small barrels which farmers used to atttach to their horses' manes to carry their own refreshments.

My Granddad, Harold John Turner, was born in 1887 on Hayling Island and was known to all as Jack Turner. He was the publican at the Farmer Inn, Catherington from 1925 until 1958. In anticipation of his retirement from the pub, he purchased Prochurch Farm from George Grant in January 1951. The deed describes the property as "parcels of land in Catherington", although they were situated on either side of London Road, just South of Lovedean Lane and Prochurch Road.

Jack and my father, John Turner were livestock dealers and hauliers. They would attend local markets such as Petersfield, Chichester, Fareham, Havant and further afield, including Winchester and Salisbury. They would purchase pigs, sheep, cattle and horses for themselves or be engaged by other local farmers to transport their livestock purchases from marketplace to their farms.

The photograph on the far left, shows Jack with his second wife, Dorothy, taken at Prochurch Farm, circa 1967. In the background are new houses (Galaxie Road) built by Faulkners Builders of Waterlooville on land that Jack had sold for redevelopment as a continuation of the Hazleton Estate.

The second photograph (near left), shows my father and brother Richard. They were keen pigeon fanciers and breeders, with a loft at Granddad's farm; they were successful in several prestigious pigeon races. Bungalows in Cotwell Avenue on the Hazleton Estate can be seen in the distance.

Sue Brett née Turner

Horndean Light Railway Staff in Cowplain Sheds

Transport of the past

The Portsdown and Horndean Light Railway was opened on March 3, 1903. The project, inspired by a Mr AW White, JP, ran from Cosham every ten minutes, for a distance of six miles to Horndean through Purbrook, Waterlooville and Cowplain, along the route of what is now the A3. Mr White is buried at Christ Church in Widley just a few yards from the route of the old railway, which before the opening of the A3M, was one of the busiest road routes in South Hampshire.

The service was amazingly frequent. It ran every 20 minutes until 11 am and every ten minutes until 9 pm. In 1910 the last train of the day would leave Cosham at 11.15 pm, reach Cowplain at 11.30 pm and would - if they had passengers - go on to Horndean. The Sunday services was good too - every ten minutes - the last tram being 11.15 pm.

The cars were powered by an electric overhead system and the power station which supplied the electric current for the line was situated in Purbrook. The engines working in conjunction with storage batteries ran all day but one or other system could be shut-off during off-peak periods.

At the Cowplain shops there was a large Car Shed where the tram cars were kept for the night. In 1910 there were 16 cars and repairs were carried out by the Company's own men. Each car seated 18 inside and 32 outside. The terminus for the light railway was just before Horndean Village at what was then the entrance of Hazleton Wood with its famous lily pond. Perhaps, because of the Light Railway, Horndean was then a holiday resort with an abundance of places where tea and refreshments could be obtained, including small cottages where they would hang out their 'Teas' signs.

The cost for the return journey from Cosham to Horndean was 8d (about 3p) but this could be reduced to 6d if the ticket was issued before 9.30 am or, for a private school or pleasure party, a whole car with a capacity of 80 children or 50 adults could be hired for 24 shillings.

Joy Smith

TRANSPORT

Horndean Light Railway

For a small country village the Car Shed building on the London Road was quite impressive. The first six trams went into service on 2nd March 1903 with 100 volunteers on board, they travelled from Cosham to Horndean then returned to the depot at Cowplain. By 1927 the trams ran down to Clarence Pier and South Parade Pier. The green and cream painted trams were known as "green cars". Eight old trams were used as shelters at the tram stops.

In the early 30s two ladies, the Miss Wests travelled on the Horndean Light Railway to work in Portsmouth. They lived in King's Road Cowplain. As the road was not made up at the time, they wore their wellington boots to the main road. Then they hid them upside down under the hedge of May Cottage on the corner of King's Road to put on again on their return journey.

Ray Piper

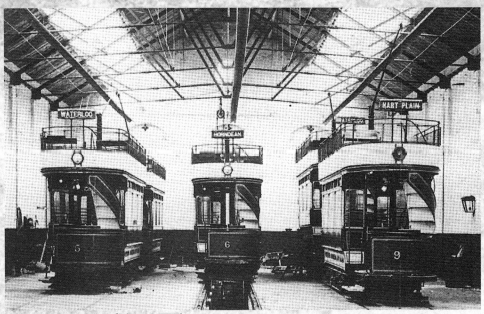

Above: *Interior of the tran depot*
Below: *No.2 Car Shed Lane in background*

Tram Depot at Cowplain, circa 1931

Typical bus that ran through Cowplain

War Memories

Eileen Gordon [née Summers], remembers hearing the declaration of war on her brother's radiogram. She lived in Hartplain Avenue at the time. She was petrified and thought she was going to be gassed immediately. Through the war she worked in a little factory in the woods at the end of Durley Avenue, making aerial torpedo releases. A few weeks ago Eileen met a man who used to retrieve the torpedoes from the Solent, a highly dangerous job.

There were soldiers camped in the Queen's Inclosure, Padnell Woods and along the main London Road. Her mother used to make pots of tea for them asking at Harcourt's grocers if they had any spare chocolate biscuits for the troops.

My friend and I went to Waterlooville to get some fish and chips, on getting off the bus at Hartplain Avenue on the way home. We were machine gunned by enemy fighter planes. Luckily, Mrs Annie Soaper ,who lived at the top of the road, took us in until the danger had passed. Mrs Soaper used to let people who lived further down Hartplain Avenue leave their bikes in her garden for a weekly charge of 2p.

The troops left the area during the night and wrote on the road in chalk "Thank you Cowplain".

In August 1940, a Heinkell 111 crash landed in Westbrook Farm in Park Lane. The farmer, Mr Bob Powell, marched the pilot and his navigator at the point of his shot gun to the Foden Works garage on the main road in Cowplain to wait for the authorities to come and arrest them.

When I was about 13 and attending, Cowplain Secondary Senior School, I joined the Cadet Force based at the school, where all the weapons were stored, rifles, stem guns and a Lewis gun. One Sunday we were picked up at the school and taken to Lord Woolston's Estate, just outside of Rowlands Castle. We practiced manoeuvres all day and when we had finished we were dropped off at home, complete with rifles. As the school was closed, we had the rifles all weekend and I had to walk to school on Monday morning with my rifle over my arm.

Two of the N.C.O.s were John and Tom Hood, whose father was the village cobbler.

No health and safety in those days.

John Goble

War and Peace Christmas Pudding

Ingredients:
8ozs flour, 8ozs bread crumbs, 4ozs suet, 4ozs dried fruit, 1 tsp. mixed spice, 8ozs grated raw carrot and ltsp. bicarbonate of soda.
Method:
Mix all the ingredients together and turn into a well-greased pudding bowl. The bowl should not be more than two-thirds full. Boil or steam for at least 2 hours. This pudding was made in Canada during the First World War. It makes a good wartime Christmas Pudding.

Chocolate Cake

Ingredients:
8ozs flour, 2 tsp. baking powder, 1oz Bourville Cocoa, 2ozs fat, l or 2tbls. dried egg, 2ozs sugar, 3 saccharin tablets, a little water and a few drops of vanilla essence.
Method:
Sieve flour, baking powder and cocoa together. Cream fat, egg and sugar, add dry ingredients alternately with the saccharins [dissolved in warm milk, water and essence] and mix well. Bake in a moderate oven for about 50 minutes.

Eggless sponge pudding

Ingredients:
6ozs self raising flour or plain flour with 1 tsp. of baking powder, 1-2ozs margarine or cooking fat, 2ozs sugar, 1tbls. Golden Syrup, ½ tsp. bicarbonate of soda, 1 dsp. vinegar, milk too mix.
Method:
Sift flour, rub in margarine or cooking fat, add sugar
and golden syrup. Blend bicarb. with vinegar add other ingredients with enough milk to make a sticky consistency. Put into a greased basin and cover with a plate or margarine paper. Steam for 1½ hours. Serve with fruit or jam.
Variation:
Use 5ozs flour and loz of cocoa powder.

Derek Harris spent the war at 41 Kings Road, Cowplain as a child. We had a lot of fun with the soldiers parked all alone the A3 and the side roads. They used to let us play on their tanks and lorries.

The ladies of Cowplain invited some of the troops to have meals with them and also to have baths.

When the plane crashed in Park Lane, my grandfather [Charles West], as a voluntary policeman/fire man, was put on duty at the site to stop people taking souvenirs. There was also a collision between a double-decker bus and a tank that went into the back.

An air raid siren was attached to the corner of the Foden works and was still being tested in the 1960s.

Cowplain men who died in the two world Wars

1914-1918
Private Frederick Budden
Sgt. William Coddington
Petty Officer Telegraphist Ernest Gamblen RN
Private Ernest Reed 1 Hants
Private Arthur Stone ¼ WILTS
Private William Taylor 6 Wilts
Chief Arificer Albert Wilkes RN

1939-1945
Flying Officer Thomas Cooper RAF
Leading Aircraftsman Albert Ayling RAF
Sgt Pilot Charles Ayling RAF
C.E.R.A Frederick Barratt RN
Stoker George Blythe RN
Gunner Eric Cattermole RA
Lieutenant Ronald Chalk RNVR
Sergeant Dennis Chappell RAFVR
Cpl Trevor Crowe RM
Private William Evans
P.O. Stoker William Folds RN

Lance Corporal Albert Gait X Hants
Leading Seaman Adolphis Galipeau RN
Seargant Frank Gander RAFVR
Sapper Harold Gander 2/11 Field Coy
Petty Officer Francis Goodchild RNR
CPO Charles Green RN
Bombadier Frederick Haworth
Lieutenant Albert House RN
Flt Sgt Engineer Albert House RAF
Warrant Officer Walter Hudson RAFVR
Stoker Edwin Jerrum
Private Gerald Pettingwell
Trooper Bertram Prentice RAC
Sergeant Harold Ralph RA
Leading Cook Frederick Ransome RN
Warrant Officer Class 1 Fred Sargent RAOC
Able Seaman George Stowers RN
Gunner Roy Tanner RA
Private Oswald White

_____

George Bolt
Henry Hayward

V.E. Day party in Cowplain

It is nice to end this book on
a happy note.

Cowplain celebrated with
lots of streeet parties.

TRICORN

BOOKS

www.tricornbooks.co.uk